WOMEN
in the
Martial Arts

edited by

Carol A. Wiley

North Atlantic Books
Berkeley, California

Women in the Martial Arts

ISBN 1-55643-136-8

Published by
North Atlantic Books
P.O. Box 12327
Berkeley, California 94712

This is issue #46 in the *Io* series.

Cover and book design by Paula Morrison
Printed in the United States of America

Cover photographs: top left, photographer unknown; top right, Stephen Long; bottom, Gary Louie.

Grateful acknowledgement is made to the following people for permission to reproduce their photographs: Maru Anthony (Laurie Cahn), Linda Boan (Debby Kirkman), Harvey Brunner (Wendy Whited), Gon Buurman (Lydia Zijdel), Grayson James (Wendy Palmer), Terry Lee (Janet Gee), Stephen Long (Janet Aalfs), Gary Louie (Elizabeth Hedricks), Dixie Paussa (Michelle Dwyer), John Rios (Carol Wiley), Carol Spier (Maria Doest).

Women in the Martial Arts is sponsored by the Society for the Study of Native Arts and Sciences, a nonprofit educational corporation whose goals are to develop an educational and crosscultural perspective linking various scientific, social, and artistic fields; to nurture a holistic view of arts, sciences, humanities, and healing; and to publish and distribute literature on the relationship of mind, body, and nature.

Table of Contents

INTRODUCTION

Carol A. Wiley

"The actions of the sports (in Aikido, *waza*) have no special value, but rather, the value is within the individual who chooses to develop her/his talents."
Kuroiwa Yoshio Sensei[1]

The value of the martial arts is not in the perfectly executed front kick or hip throw; the value is in how people use the training to develop themselves. Several essays in this book refer to the martial arts as a mirror for life, a way to see oneself. Challenges that arise in training often arise elsewhere in life where they are muddled by surrounding complications. If a person finds herself collapsing under a strong attack in class, she also may be collapsing when mentally or emotionally pushed in life. Learning to be strong in training can translate to being strong when faced with life's other challenges. In this way, the value of martial arts training is the empowerment of self.

The themes of empowerment and willingness to face challenges appear in many of the essays in this book. These twenty-three essays present perspectives on the martial arts from women who have been training from seven to twenty years. These women represent twelve different martial arts, and many have trained in more than one style. This book is the first to collect the writings of women who have this depth and breadth of experience in the martial arts.

---

[1]Kuroiwa Yoshio Sensei, translated by Joel Roth, "Appearance and Reality," *Fighting Woman News*, Winter 1985.

Why focus on the perspectives of women? Are their perspectives necessarily different from men's perspectives? Although each individual brings unique experiences and beliefs to the martial arts, women often face different challenges in their training. I was talking to several people about this book, and one woman, who is not a martial artist, asked if the martial arts were different for women. I replied that I thought so because women are usually socialized differently. Another woman, a contributor to this book and an instructor, agreed. She asked, "How many men in class have you seen throw their hands above their heads, shrink back, and say 'Don't hurt me'? I've certainly seen women do it." Women must also more often deal with issues of sexual assault and abuse. Thus by focusing on the perspectives of women, this book offers a different view into a world traditionally dominated and written about by men.

Several essays touch on the differences between women and men as beginners in the martial arts, pointing out that lack of physical confidence is a drawback, yet women are also often physically looser and more flexible than men. This looseness can help prevent injury. Flexibility can make techniques, especially kicks, easier to learn. But the important point is that regardless of where a person begins, she or he can become proficient, perhaps even excel, in the martial arts given the proper internal motivation and external encouragement and instruction.

The martial arts are often automatically linked to self-defense, and some of the essays discuss self-defense. Self-defense is more a mental attitude than a specific set of techniques, and the martial arts are only one possible way to develop that attitude. As one contributor says, "It's not enough to learn that you can hurt someone twenty-three different ways in five seconds flat if they jump you. If you don't feel good about yourself, if you're not confident within yourself, if you haven't got a sense of having a right to the territory that you occupy, then no amount of technique, no bag of little tricks is going to help, because you aren't going to react properly when push comes to shove." Even when the martial arts are used for self-defense, this doesn't necessarily mean a swift kick to the groin. The goal at the highest level of martial

2

arts training is the peaceful resolution of conflict. Good martial arts training provides a complete range of options, adaptable to any situation.

Although the value of martial arts training is not in any particular approach, each martial art does have its own emphasis and strengths. A martial art might emphasize traditional training, self-defense, sport and competition, spiritual development, or particular types of movements. Different approaches are suitable for different people, depending on variables of personality, physical build, and background. A particular approach may be successful for a person at one point in life but not at another. For example, I trained in Tae Kwon Do for more than seven years. The direct, linear movements taught me physical confidence and strength that I previously lacked and honed my focus and concentration. When I began training in Aikido, I brought these skills with me but had to face another, for me, more difficult situation: connection with a partner. Had I started with Aikido instead of Tae Kwon Do, I feel it is likely I would not have stuck with it. I needed to learn the physical confidence before I could face the emotional issues that have arisen in my Aikido training where I must constantly work with partners and cannot escape into the solitude of form practice.

Many of the martial arts practiced today were developed in the 19th and 20th centuries from the ancient Asian fighting arts. The martial arts evolved to fit into modern society, leaving behind many of the ancient combat skills and offering a training more relevant to modern life. Values related to the martial arts have also evolved. For example, the values of the Samurai of Japan included fighting and dying for one's lord with unflinching loyalty. Today we (Americans in particular) believe in thinking for ourselves, not unquestioningly following someone else. But we can take the Samurai's value of loyalty and apply it to ourselves. Loyalty to oneself means having the courage to make decisions and follow through on them, having self-confidence and self-esteem.

The martial arts are often called the way of the warrior, for the strengths of the warrior are courage and discipline. The warrior need no longer fight physical battles. Our warrior's courage and our belief in self will help us win the most important battles: the battles within, the battles against fears and frustrations, hopelessness, despair, cynicism, and self-limiting concepts. But life is more than just a battle, and the best martial artists are more than warriors: They are sages, seekers of knowledge, always learning, always growing. I hope this book will expand the knowledge of both martial artists and non-martial artists. Here are the experiences of twenty-three women who have used their martial arts training to tap and develop potential most people don't know they have.

COMING HOME: T'AI CHI CH'UAN AS A PATH OF HEALING

Jody Curley

Let me tell you about a homecoming: a woman coming home to her body.

I must begin, however, with her exile.

The woman whose story this is—let me call her Brenda—is a survivor of childhood abuse. She abandoned her body, in a figurative if not a literal sense, when she was very young because her body was simply too dangerous a place to stay. Brenda became a homeless refugee of a war fought by her parents on the battlefields of her family home and her own vulnerable psyche. She dissociated from her bodily experience of life when the trauma—the physical, emotional, and sexual abuse—became too much for her child's mind to integrate. Brenda became a disembodied soul and spirit, living principally in her head, numb to most of her emotional experience, moving through the world in a body she sometimes was aware of hating but most often just ignored. Her body was, to her, the primary vehicle of her betrayal. She found it unworthy of positive regard at best and utterly repulsive at worst.

Brenda was born into a family in which crisis was the ongoing rhythm of "normalcy." Both her parents had been abused as children, and they had grown to adulthood without acknowledging or healing their childhood wounds. They unconsciously passed on

their familial legacies of pain and shame to their children.

Brenda's father was prone to unpredictable, explosive rages and deadening depressions. Brenda's mother accommodated the abusive behavior of her husband out of a core conviction that she deserved nothing better. She was alienated from her own body, communicating to Brenda and her sisters ambivalence about the whole matter of womanhood. Brenda saw little reason to want to grow up to be a woman; it seemed a sad, helpless, and hopeless thing to be.

Brenda's father also held ambivalence toward women. His mother had abused him, although he never consciously confronted the ways in which she had hurt him. His mother was a primary caregiver for Brenda when she was very young. Other family members tell Brenda that this grandmother was often cruel to Brenda, cruel verging on sadistic. Brenda does not remember.

The defenses of the human psyche are extraordinary: how our minds protect us when there is no help available; how we numb ourselves to what feels unendurable; how we forget in order to survive.

Brenda remembers the sweet, ripe bananas with their dappled brown and yellow skins in the bottom drawer of her grandmother's white kitchen cabinet. She remembers slouching through the hot, buzzing summer afternoons in the striped canvas lounge chair on her grandmother's screen porch. She remembers snapping off crisp stalks of rhubarb in the backyard patch; she remembers pressing her hot cheek against the cool, smooth lip of the porcelain tub with the fancy feet. These things she remembers as clearly as if she were three years old today. But Brenda has almost no memory of her grandmother or of how her grandmother treated her. She has a single visual image of a fat woman with blue-tinted hair and bright spots of rouge on her cheeks, laughing. Brenda has been told that her grandmother was often laughing at her—taunting, teasing, baiting, deceiving. Brenda does not remember.

There is more Brenda does not remember. She has huge gaps in her memory throughout the first fifteen years of her life. She has little in the way of visual images to show her adult self what was done to her and by whom. She does have powerful body memories, nightmares, and the psychological profile of an incest survivor. She has a constellation of beliefs, feelings, and behaviors that reflect the violation of *self* she experienced as a child. For many years, Brenda engaged in a variety of forms of self-punishment, attempting to make her amorphous, pervasive internal pain external, visible, palpable, understandable: "Oh, thank god; now I have a *real reason* to hurt as much as I do ... and now I am in control of my hurting."

Then, after some thirty years of exile from her body and her self, Brenda began the return home. She began to study T'ai Chi Ch'uan.

Brenda saw a man doing T'ai Chi Ch'uan in a park one summer morning, his limbs gliding so slowly and gracefully in the sunlight that filtered through the leaves of the old oaks encircling him that she did a most uncharacteristic thing: She stopped and stared for minutes, transfixed. She admired people who used their bodies fluidly, elegantly. Her own body had always seemed so clumsy and ridiculously unresponsive that physical grace occupied, for her, the realm of myth. Yet, something about what this man was doing, while exotic and unusual, seemed attainable in the real world. These movements looked peaceful, private, and *easy* . . . a physical activity so slow that she wondered if even her awkward, uncoordinated body could do it. She thought there was a chance.

So Brenda enrolled in a T'ai Chi Ch'uan class. She hated walking into a gathering of people she didn't know and exposing the awful inadequacy of her body for everyone to see. She was determined, however, that she would tolerate the class environment just long enough to learn a sequence of movements that she could do in the private retreat of her living room. That would be the end of formal study; she would simply practice by herself thereafter.

The first surprise for Brenda was that it was very difficult to move her body in a way that looked *easy*. The second surprise was that, whatever difficulty she experienced, many of the other students in class seemed to struggle even more than she did. The third surprise was that she liked the class and she loved the novel sensation of warmth and aliveness apparently generated by the sequence of movements she was learning. The embodied sensation of well-being was so radically different from the dull lethargy she usually experienced that she was hooked. She wanted more of it.

And so Brenda's life has gone since that first day of class some ten years ago—wanting more of it and finding ways to get it. The world has changed for Brenda, because Brenda changed. She committed herself to a discipline that gradually facilitates the integration of mind, body, and spirit. She began to experience what it is to feel moments of *wholeness*. She awakened to her sexuality, an aspect of her experience to which she had been closed and numb. She began to feel like a woman and to like it. She entered therapy and began the intense work of identifying the sources of her psychic pain, of reclaiming all the parts of herself she had long before disowned as shameful and worthless. There were months during this phase of her inner work that were dark and bleak, and she wondered at times if she would survive the remembering necessary to her healing. T'ai Chi Ch'uan was a centering and grounding practice for her during this time, an oasis of relative ease and rest when all the rest of her life seemed arid and toilsome.

When Brenda began her T'ai Chi Ch'uan study, she had no thought of using it to heal her inner wounds. She was not particularly conscious of the injuries she had sustained in childhood. The pain she felt seemed constant and inevitable to her—the normal ground of her existence, not amenable to change.

What Brenda did not know when she came to T'ai Chi Ch'uan was that *awareness* is one of the most powerful healing forces available to human beings. The purpose of meditative techniques developed and practiced for millennia is to cultivate conscious awareness as a path to integration of all aspects of the personal self, culminating in an experience of union or oneness with what may be called The Way of Things, or Tao, or All-That-Is, or The Divine. When we are in this state of consciousness, we know our own intrinsic perfection with the entirety of our beings. In this state, there is no injury. We are healed and whole.

T'ai Chi Ch'uan requires that awareness be consciously focused in the pelvis. The implications of this for students with wounded sexuality are significant. As students attempt to move with proper body mechanics and alignment, which requires consistently attending to what the hips and pelvis are doing, T'ai Chi Ch'uan players like Brenda may discover they have been "frozen" in their hips and pelvis. The breathing cultivated through T'ai Chi Ch'uan study is diaphragmatic breathing; the breath is sunk from the chest to the lower abdomen. The center of breath and movement is established in the *tan tien*, the energetic center below the navel that corresponds to the *hara* or the second *chakra*, the seat of sexual energy. T'ai Chi Ch'uan practitioners often find it challenging to focus their attention on the *tan tien*, particularly in the beginning phases of study. Many people have little or no conscious awareness of this part of the body.

As Brenda's T'ai Chi Ch'uan practice increased her flexibility and muscle acuity by slowly and persistently bringing her attention back to how she moved her hips and pelvis, she discovered she had been both physically "locked" and energetically blocked in her pelvic region, as if the years of overt and covert abuse had activated a self-protective shut-down of pelvic awareness. Brenda's T'ai Chi Ch'uan practice provided a non-threatening way to feel and use her pelvis more consciously than she ever had. As she gradually came home to this part of her body, she began to feel relaxed, safe, confident, and competent in her life outside the practice room. As she moved her body more gracefully, fluidly, and powerfully, she felt more able to express grace, fluidity, and power in her daily life.

The dramatic and direct connections between her bodily experience and her psychological state repeatedly astounded Brenda. She now understood that being physically centered, balanced, and grounded inevitably contributed to an emotional state in which she felt relaxed, calm, and stable. She realized for the first time the literal truths expressed by common phrases like "pulling my own weight," "standing on my own two feet," "having a leg to stand on." She also began to acknowledge more fully the womanliness of the body she lived in, to be able to look in the mirror, and to like what she saw. She started to feel a previously unknown respect for the magnificent responsiveness of the physical form she inhabited, the body that had served her all her life as she had ignored it or hated it or punished it. She felt a surprising new desire to *care* for her body and to live in a mutually affirming partnership with it.

Brenda had been hurt by both men and women when she was a child. She had grown into adulthood distrusting people, male and female. As she began the two-person practice of push hands in her T'ai Chi Ch'uan class, she was confronted by the anxiety of being in a close physical relationship with another person. It was equally uncomfortable for her to play with women and men. To her great good fortune, she encountered teachers of both sexes who modeled the ability to establish workable relationships with either men or women. Her teachers conveyed to her the very real possibility of generating physical power regardless of size or degree of muscularity.

Brenda began to perceive one of the great beauties of her art: T'ai Chi Ch'uan does not rely on muscular strength to be effective; instead it trains sensitivity to the flow of movement in an interaction while using the intrinsic alignment of the skeletal structure in relationship to gravity. IN RELATIONSHIP: these words became of paramount consideration as Brenda continued her push hands study. She needed to learn to stay in conscious relationship with her body while simultaneously relating to another person. In time, she found herself making techniques *work*. She started to feel *strong* in a way she had never considered possible—not a muscle-bound, static strength but a resilient, dynamic strength that felt increasingly easy and powerful.

As Brenda's trust in her body's ability to do what she asked increased, her fear of being in close physical relationship with others dissipated. She began to enjoy the contact, to marvel at the differences in the bodies of those she played with, to experiment with the techniques she had learned, to be creative in her responses to her partners. She began to pay more attention to the unfolding changes in the moment-by-moment interactions with her fellow students and less attention to her habitual self-judgements and anxieties about being harmed. She became far less *self*-conscious; her consciousness expanded to include awareness of the reality of the human beings she stood in face-to-face and body-to-body relationship with. Her former fears transformed into *curiosity*, and she began to truly play, to have fun as she learned.

From push hands play, Brenda was persuaded, much to her surprise, to try free fighting. Her teachers taught it as an exercise of conscious awareness and precise control rather than an opportunity to inflict pain. Brenda discovered T'ai Chi Ch'uan free fighting to be a laboratory for the study of human relationship. She noticed almost every relationship dynamic possible arising during free fighting, including emotional states such as survival fear, rage, the desire to hurt another, the desire to **win** at all costs, the desire to collapse and give up and stop trying ... all the "heavy stuff." But it was there as an opportunity to make choices, to make workable responses rather then fear-driven reactions, and to experience how we are actually *safer* when we stay in touch with the emotions we often deny or repress.

Sometimes, when free fighting, Brenda felt physical pain. Initially, she experienced relief when she felt the pain of a penetrating punch or kick. This pain was understandable—it was direct, overt, clear, and undeniable. As her training continued and as Brenda and her classmates became more skillful, she began to acknowledge more fully her real fear of bodily harm, and she gradually reframed her perception of pain.

Brenda learned that pain need not be synonymous with injury. She learned that it is a sensation providing useful feedback; that she could learn from the pain and adapt her responses to make the free fighting relationship work more effectively for her. Pain became a teacher she respected. She learned to be patient with herself when she felt awkward or inept; to return to the principles of T'ai Chi Ch'uan movement when she felt her anxiety or her desire to perform well impair her ability to simply do what was called for in any given moment. She learned to increasingly stay *present*, rather than judging what she had just done or anticipating what was to come. And, once again, she found her T'ai Chi Ch'uan practice slipping out of the studio into other areas of her life. Her practice became something she was always doing, whether she was in the practice room or not.

Brenda now says that she knows T'ai Chi Ch'uan is a life-long study. She views it as a system of physical exercise, a tool for stress reduction, a method of meditation, a training in self-defense—and she views these components as parts of a greater whole. T'ai Chi Ch'uan is ultimately, for Brenda, an art of self transformation.

As written in the T'ai Chi Ch'uan Classics, the solo form is the way of knowing oneself; the two-person practice is the way of knowing others. T'ai Chi Ch'uan is an art of *knowing*, an art of relationship: relationship with self, with other beings, and with the universe we live in. Knowing who we are as we move through our lives, we reclaim the parts of ourselves we have disowned and cast off into the shadow realms of our psyches. Like Brenda, we heal. We trust our right to fully inhabit our miraculous human bodies. We end our exile and come home to ourselves.

In My Chinese Shoes

The man is big.
Body to body
My hands find him
As my mind
Finds basic ground beneath our feet.
Sinking
Quiet
I draw up earth into my palms
Uproot him
Catch him
Turn him
Let him fall where his own wind blows
And as he goes
I look him in his
Eye of disbelief:
Now we both know
I am no longer small.

IRIMI:
GOING FOR LIFE

Wendy Palmer

When I was a young girl I loved to ride horses. I dreamed of galloping as fast as the wind astride a strong stallion with a long, flowing mane. One day that dream came true.

My friend, Lynnie, and I sneaked into the "forbidden" corral that contained her father's thoroughbred stallion, appropriately named Bridlefree. He was "fresh off the track," and they had unloaded him with a chain over his nose while he fought and reared, his nostrils flaring red inside. The men had put him in a corral and warned us not to go near it. He was "very dangerous," they said. When they left, we went to him, bringing him sugar, carrots, and lots of love and adoration. We slipped on his back and noticed how beautiful, strong, and muscled he felt compared to the mares and geldings we were accustomed to riding.

One day, I don't know why, we went for the dream. Lynnie took a trusted gelding bareback with a simple bridle, and I put only a lead rope on Bridefree's halter. We opened the corral and we were free. Lynnie and the gelding began to gallop across a field toward a tree-covered lane. Bridlefree sensed the play and took off, his thoroughbred heart and untamed spirit leaping across the field.

We hurtled toward the lane. I twisted his long mane around my hands. I wanted to stay with him no matter what happened.

I was living a dream and was determined to live it to the fullest. When we entered the lane, I had to lean way over and sometimes duck my head below my hands to avoid the branches whipping over my body. Bridlefree interpreted my position as encouragement and I felt him surge a little more, his muscles driving even harder. I could hear his breath and his hooves rhythmically pounding the earth. When I looked down at the ground moving by so fast, my head swam. I closed my eyes, tightened my grip on his mane, and pressed my body into his as much as I could. I remember trying to feel way into him. I wanted to become one with him.

The end of the lane was coming up, with a substantial right turn that led into a short narrow field. Before that moment I would have considered it impossible to take the turn at the speed we were going. Now it seemed that anything was possible. I shifted my weight, moving my head to the right side of his neck. His body responded slightly, but for me it was as if I had whispered in his ear and he had heard me. He slipped a little in the turn, but we made it and were into the open. He slowed a little and circled, stopped and began to graze. My body was trembling as I unwound Bridefree's mane from around my hand. His flanks were heaving and his coat glistened in the sun. I had embodied a dream. I sensed anything was possible.

Sixteen years later I saw Aikido for the first time. It was as if a crack in the cosmos opened and a whiff of something forgotten yet familiar passed through me. That whiff was the memory of joining with a power, physically much stronger than I, and it becoming open and receptive to my intentions. It was the feeling of flight, of giving oneself with the innocence of total love and admiration. Beauty, grace, power, surrender—all of these stirred my desire to embody the dream again. Dreams and fantasies are great. The embodiment of them is even greater.

Growing up had seemed to be a journey into fear. When I was young, getting hurt meant little while I was actively pursuing the dream. As I got older, the dream began to fade, and protecting myself—not getting hurt—became the major task. I used my mind to understand things, instead of my body to experience them. At the age of twenty-four I had read many things about

physics and existentialism. I knew and loved the Tao Te Ching, but my cells no longer moved toward and hungered after flight, grace, beauty, power, and surrender.

Then, as I saw the movements of Aikido, I felt a deep sense of coming home—a returning—like waking up and remembering the part of oneself that hungers after the experience of essential contact. The Buddhists call it *tantra*. The part that knows real satisfaction does not come from standing back and observing, but from entering the energetic vortex of universal life and breath.

My heart filled with romantic inspiration and I began training. The vast chasm between what I saw and sensed and what I could do was not entirely shocking but was extremely painful to experience. It was hard to bear the fact that all the discomfort, emotionally and physically, I experienced was brought on by me. I desperately wanted some part, however small, to belong to my partners. It really felt as if they were doing it to me. I couldn't be doing all this to myself, could I?

Not until a few years later could I appreciate, in a cognitive way, how powerful that step was—to realize, at the level of physical sensation, that we do orchestrate the situations of our discomfort. The other person is not doing it to us. Once we acknowledge this, we can begin the Aiki process of irimi: Moving into the situation, yearning for that center and essential essence, and developing deeper contact with center.

Center is the part of us that remembers we belong to the universe, the part that feels no need to protect oneself since it is not in opposition. For me, center is fed by desire, passion, and curiosity for the experience of essential contact. The trick is to allow my desire to be stronger than my fear. My aggression, which stems from my fear, pushes back my desire and makes me want to protect myself. Instead I look to yearn for the center, the way a lover yearns for the embrace of the beloved, the way a young girl might yearn to gallop bareback astride a great stallion.

WALKING THE WAY OF THE WARRIOR

Debby Kirkman

In one life I am a normal person: I am married, have a respectable job, and practice my religion. I live in a suburban house with my husband, three children, and a cat. In my other life I am a martial artist, a practitioner of the ancient martial art called Bando. It is such an important part of me that almost no obstacle will prevent me from attending class or from practicing outside of class.

Bando is the martial art of Burma. The word Bando can be translated several ways, including a way of discipline, the art of fighting, or the way of the warrior. The art is nearly two thousand years old and was developed and influenced from the constant fighting with Burma's neighbors, India, China, Tibet, and Thailand. Bando was brought from Burma to the United States in 1960 by Dr. Maung Gyi, who fought in several wars in Asia, including World War II. In 1967 he formed the American Bando Association (ABA) in tribute to American soldiers who fought in the wars of Asia, including the theaters of China, India, and Burma in World War II, the Korean War, and the Vietnam War.

Bando is not a well-known system. Because it is dedicated as a tribute to veterans, all those who enter Bando are taught that *Bando is not for sale*. No instructor can use Bando as a livelihood and no member of the ABA runs any commercial schools that teach Bando. People who teach do it for the love of the art and the students they nurture. Because of this, instructors are less pressured to promote students prematurely. Further, no student can be promoted to the level of first degree black belt without the approval of Dr. Gyi.

The system of Bando contains many styles of fighting, with both empty hand and weapon techniques. A weapon is seen as an extension of the hand. The weapons taught include the kukri (a short, curved sword), long sword, long staff, short stick, and police baton. Of all the weapons taught, the kukri has special significance: The symbol of Bando contains two crossed kukris, representing the exchange of knowledge between East and West. In this spirit, Bando continues to incorporate new knowledge, regardless of its origins.

Bando contains three major styles of fighting: low, middle, and high. In the low style, techniques are used to seriously injure an opponent. In the middle style, techniques are used to disable an opponent's weapons, such as the hands and feet. In the high style, the opponent is never directly attacked. Techniques are used to redirect the opponent's attack until the opponent gives up or injures himself or herself.

All aspects of fighting, whether with empty hand or with a weapon, are taught using the same set of principles. Stepping, for example, is done to the side or at angles, not forward or backward. Movement is smooth and circular. Defense is emphasized; attacks are made from a position of safety. Speed and perfect technique are more important than strength. Once students master the basic principles and reach the first level, they begin to learn one or more of Bando's animal systems. An animal system uses fighting techniques that emulate an animal, such as boar, bull, panther, tiger, cobra, python, scorpion, and eagle. Students select a system based on the desired fighting style and their own physical attributes. A student of the bull system, typically of great bulk, would not be suitable for a cat system, such as panther, which requires more agility.

I have studied Bando since 1984. We have a very small club, with a typical class size of ten to twelve students attending each Monday night. There is no separation of belts; all students are taught the same material. The advanced students learn more of the fine points of a technique while the beginning students learn the basic principles and their application to the technique being taught. The discipline required to attend class and to practice has come from my love of the art and from the inspiration of my teachers, Joe Manley and Errol Younger. Both are masters of the Bando system and were among the earliest students of Dr. Gyi. I attend whether I am healthy or sick, able or disabled. One reason I make this effort is that the physical exercise always makes me feel better than I would have felt without it. The other reason is that the knowledge shared in class by the teachers can be gained only by being there; some points are always lost by getting notes second hand from another student.

One of the major disabilities I've had to deal with while attending class is pregnancy.[1] My first child was born shortly before I joined class and since joining, I've had two additional children. Because of the obvious risks, I had to refrain from sparring during the times I was pregnant. Other than this, however, I continued to train, although I had to train at 80 percent capacity, rather than 100 percent. Training kept me fit during pregnancy, and I'm sure that it kept me healthier than had I refrained from exercise. Of course, some exercises, such as push-ups, are impossible when there is an obstacle between one's back and the floor. Pregnancy, however, did not preclude my ability to continue to learn and practice new techniques. If I had quit class during pregnancy, I would not only have lost the opportunity of learning, but would also have lost ground from lack of continued practice. Also, practically, pregnancy never protects someone from danger. For self defense, one should be able to respond in whatever condition one is in, including any present disabilities. Otherwise, why learn to fight?

The major effect pregnancy had on technique was in kicking. Because the change in body shape is gradual, I was able to compensate for a different weight distribution. After about six or sev-

---

[1]Exercise during pregnancy, of course, should be discussed with one's doctor. I'm lucky that there were no problems that prevented me from continuing to practice; other conditions may prevent active training.

en months, however, my stomach started getting in the way and I couldn't easily raise my leg to kick high targets. The most difficult part, as it turns out, is the transition from pregnancy to post-pregnancy. Suddenly, my weight distribution was vastly different, and I wasn't balanced any more. Another side effect of post-pregnancy has come about from taking care of babies. Carrying children keeps my arm muscles strong. Giving the children rides on my feet helps keep my legs strong. Although I have less time to set aside for exercise, I still keep pretty fit just through day-to-day activities.

The other disability I've had to adapt to was a major injury to my left knee. In 1987, while practicing outdoors with the class, I slipped on the grass and tore a ligament in my knee. This made my knee unstable, and I could not use it for support. Moving the wrong way, or trying to stand on the left leg, often ended with me on the ground. Thanks to the modern development of sports medicine, I was able to get reconstructive surgery to correct the problem. Healing took two years.

Every disability, though, can be channeled into new ability. For the first six weeks after surgery, I was on crutches. So, I went

21

to class on crutches, and either trained in a chair or while standing on one leg. Using crutches strengthened my arms considerably, and I became pretty good at punching while sitting down. For the next year, I had to wear a leg brace continuously and not use the leg other than for walking. During this time, I learned a great deal of balance on the right leg. I became very good at punching while standing on one leg! The second year I was allowed to train fully, but while wearing a brace. The brace was heavy and stiff, but it forced me to make the left leg stronger. I have always liked kicking techniques, but this disability forced me to train my hand techniques to be better than they had ever been.

The greatest lesson I learned while disabled was that training is not only physical but also mental. Joe Manley taught me to train mentally, to go over techniques and moves in my mind. I was amazed to see that, because I trained mentally, I did improve even when I couldn't exercise. Mental training can be done anywhere, anytime. Although I am not disabled now, there are times when it is not possible for me to exercise and practice the lessons taught in class. In these times, I can still practice mentally, and so improve my understanding of Bando.

Bando is the way of discipline. The discipline to train continuously comes naturally with the desire to learn continuously. I've learned a great deal, as a student of Bando, about the meaning of overcoming one's obstacles and turning them into strengths.

GOLDEN PHOENIX RISES

Michelle Dwyer

The study, practice, and teaching of martial arts has enriched my life on every level. The most profound effects have been my psychological and spiritual growth. The Taoist masters say only one thing counts in this life and that is to look deeply into the structure of your being. It is this aspect of the discipline, enabling one to know oneself, that holds the most fascination for me.

My first efforts to know myself came in my early twenties with Kundalini and Hatha Yoga, which gave me a good foundation in breath control and centering energy. A few years later I became enchanted with Tai Chi Chuan, an art that suited my personality. Tai Chi Chuan was more active and social than Yoga, while still having a meditative aspect.

Tai Chi is a living art that has been passed down through many generations. It is a therapeutic exercise and meditation and also a sport and fighting system. There is an old Chinese saying that the person who practices Tai Chi regularly over time will have the pliability of a child, the health of a lumberjack, and the peace of mind of a sage. It is this gradual and inevitable change that my pursuit of martial arts has wrought in me that I would like to share.

Though a very physical and active person in my youth and school years, I never had any formal athletic training. I was very

self-conscious, and my movements in public were stiff and uncomfortable. The precise movements of Tai Chi Chuan offered a wonderful framework to learn strength, grace, and confidence. My knees were once weak and went through painful periods. Now they don't complain after six or more hours of training some days. I walk with the easy, natural grace of an athlete. My self-confidence is communicated in body language that makes me an unlikely target for hassling.

The fluid movements of Tai Chi are attainable by people of all ages and abilities. As a soft, internal martial art, Tai Chi teaches strength through gentleness. Growth is measured in inner awareness, so there are no tests, belts, or ranking systems. One learns to compete with self, stretching limits day by day. Good health is the first goal of Tai Chi, meaning a vibrant balance of body, mind, and spirit. The art has given me a fit and attractive body and has protected me from colds or flus while working with the public for many years. True self-defense! Tai Chi is especially effective in aiding arthritis, high blood pressure, lower back pain, and stress.

The strong mind/body connection created by repeated practice of Tai Chi is an added bonus. The mind memorizes the slow and tranquil movements step by step. All the theories and philosophy of Tai Chi Chuan must be made real in the body. Memory is sharpened and the ability to focus the mind is increased. Concentration on the calm, flowing movements forms a habit of awareness that carries over to every action, even in our daily lives. My involvement in learning and teaching these physical arts nurtures and supports creativity in other parts of my life, one feeding the other, reflecting life's fullness. Training provides a mirror for individual reflections of character, giving the student the opportunity to question certain aspects of self such as stubbornness, judgementalism, jealousy, perseverance, and victimization. Often if I criticize a classmate's efforts to grasp a fine point, the same area is precisely what I should improve in my techniques! Tai Chi also teaches humility. One can practice forever and still be a beginner. Watching in the mirror of practice, one can develop a sense of humor and learn to be patient with oneself. The mind becomes flexible enough to learn from each situation and each person it meets.

The opportunity to increase spiritual awareness while exercising is another benefit of Tai Chi. When performing Tai Chi, the movements are like white clouds floating across the blue sky. The spirit of awareness is like a hawk circling effortlessly in the blue sky but ever ready to dive on the rabbit or mouse. Though slow and gentle, the style demands perfect balance and absolute coordination of body and mind. Total awareness of breath and movement help create a meditative state that frees the spirit to grow and blossom. With this spiritual awareness comes a sense of personal power and worth, calmness and security. This well-rounded discipline is very life giving, life affirming, for the individual and for society as a whole. The first step to the success of any relationship, and indeed to world peace, is to know and love yourself.

The principles of Tai Chi are based on the world's oldest philosophy, Taoism, and offer a life-time goal of enlightenment. Taoism teaches that we are individually responsible for our state of being, physical, mental, emotional, and spiritual. The human body is the microcosm, the universe the macrocosm. The spiritual, mental, and physical body must be united, then the whole person and the universe can be unified. This is the goal of meditation and the ultimate goal of Tai Chi. Needless to say, this takes many years of practice. My teacher once said that training is like rowing a boat upstream. If one stops rowing one doesn't just stay there, one starts slipping downstream.

From a shy and private individual, I have bloomed into an active and public teacher. I treasure the positive changes training has brought to my life and am eager to share these jewels of the Orient with my culture. This semester, I have nearly one hundred students at the two local colleges where I have been teaching for five years. The great benefits of the art are reflected back to me in the healthy, happy mirror of my students' faces.

My training has also brought adventure to my life, taking me around the globe and to many interesting cultural events in my own area. One of my students worked for an airline and obtained a free round-trip ticket to Hong Kong for me. I went by myself to see the other side of the world and practiced at dawn with people in the parks. Another long awaited dream came true last summer, when I was accepted to teach kung fu and Hsing Yi at FIST '90 (Feminist International Summer Training) in Holland. This trip was my very first visit to Europe and a chance to meet women from all over the globe. Fortunately they all spoke my first language, English, and my second language, martial arts.

In addition to Tai Chi, I am a long time student of Northern Shaolin Kung Fu and Hsing Yi with the Chinese Physical Association. Usually I am the only woman training in class. In the 30 years of the school, I am the only woman to learn the complete Northern Shaolin System. This club performs Lion Dances at events in the extensive Asian community of the Bay Area. This Chinese folk dance brings good luck and prosperity to weddings, birthdays, schools, businesses, and the New Year parade. So my martial arts training has given me a healthy, calm, vibrant life full of friends and associates in my neighborhood, and nation, and around the world.

The phoenix is a symbol of rebirth. The Golden Phoenix Rises is step #15 in my Yang style Family Set Tai Chi Chuan. Tai Chi opened the door of the martial arts world for me. It has taught me to challenge myself and succeed. It has helped me grow in many ways I never would have imagined. The biggest lesson my training has taught me is that the best fighting is with oneself.

MY JOURNEY WITH AIKIDO

Wendy Whited

Why study Aikido? I'm not a fighter, I hate confrontations, and I'm a dedicated pacifist. Pain is not a feeling I particularly enjoy or seek out, but I train in Aikido three to four days a week and have even studied in Japan.

Considering my situation, spending all this time seems even stranger; I don't need to defend myself. I live in the country and rarely lock my doors. The most dangerous situation I face is walking into my seventh grade classroom the first three weeks of school. I have never been attacked where I had to defend myself from someone who truly wanted to hurt me. Do I study with the hope that someday I'll get to use it? No way! The idea of being attacked gives me the willies. Did I hope to collect trophies from competitions or become the best in my *dojo*, city, or state? That's a waste of time in Aikido since my chosen style doesn't allow tournaments. Then why do this Aikido stuff?

I was looking for an art that would encourage my personal growth, not my competitive edge. I showed horses for fifteen years and during that time I realized that competition rarely allows people to work together or even to coach each other. How could you justify helping a fellow competitor when she might turn around and beat you in the next class? It is unrealistic to expect people to give you the fighting secrets that allow them to bring home the trophies they want to win. Competition also has a way of warping a person's view of herself. If you win, people tend to see you as an "important person," but if you lose, you're not worth worrying about. I'd had enough of being a wonderful person when I won and no one when I lost.

When I found Aikido, I was amazed there were no tournaments. I knew other arts competed so I was thrilled not to have to worry about winning and losing. In Aikido you work with your partner, taking turns attacking and defending. From the first day I joined the *dojo*, people were eager for me to get better. The faster I improved, the more fun my partner could have with me. I thought this was great. People went out of their way to teach me and stayed after class to help me get ready for my first test. It seemed so easy at first. My partner tried to grab my wrist, with a quick turn I took her balance, then she hit the floor. Boy, was this fun.

After a great beginning and a triple promotion, Aikido suddenly became harder to do. Senior students were still happy to work with me, but my partners weren't cooperating as they had when I was a white belt. People were willing to be patient with a novice, but as I gained expertise, more was expected. Going to the *dojo* became more frustrating. I had found my competition: Myself. I realized I wanted Aikido to be easy, but I found it wasn't going to be easy. I couldn't blame my problems on my partners; I had to look in the mirror. I had to stop expecting my partners to fall for any technique, no matter how poorly executed, and instead look at why they didn't fall. When I set up my partners so that they had no option except to fall, I had made my first leap in Aikido.

When practice became more difficult, it was part of the growing I had wanted, but I didn't care for the frustration. It was hard to realize how much work I was going to have to put into my practice, and I wasn't sure at first that I wanted to continue. That was when self-discipline entered the scene. Until that time, as with most people, my motivation had always been external. Do something unpleasant because your parents or boss said you had to do it. Suddenly I had to decide if I wanted to continue. No one

was going to make me or call and ask me to come to practice. I decided to continue.

After this, Aikido should have been great, but of course the next wall waited for me. I trained harder. I jogged when I didn't get to the *dojo*. Now I could throw and put my partner down pretty hard. However, that was all I cared about. I didn't think about how my partner felt about being smashed to the floor, and I developed a reputation as one scary person. The only people I wanted to train with were the ones I could throw easily. People started to shy away from me on the mat, and I started feeling the loss of connection with my fellow Aikidoists. I didn't want to fall (read that as "lose"). I would reverse my partner to escape falling. After a few months, I realized I was competing, exactly what I had joined Aikido hoping to avoid. What to do?

Fortunately, I had a teacher who helped me through this period. Sensei wasn't impressed with my power and suggested I start feeling what I was doing to my partner. I began to relax and not worry about whether my partner fell. The initial movements became fascinating and my throws became smoother. Controlling my breathing became important, and the competitive edge just disappeared. As my throws became gentler, partners were more eager to train with me. I again had friends, not enemies, to work with.

Where my Aikido will go from here is hard to say. I hope it will become more intuitive, maybe even more spiritual and less connected with physical power. As I watch my seniors, I see a person attack, something happens that appears effortless, and then the attacker flies through the air. That's what I want, my Aikido to appear effortless.

As my Aikido has become more confident, I find my personal life has become more secure. I'm not competing with my fellow teachers for recognition; I just do a good job and it shows. I don't worry about how I can impress my friends; I think about how I can help them. I now know that I study Aikido to become the best person I can be. As with my Aikido, I can't predict where my life is heading, but I'm sure enjoying the journey.

A MIRROR FOR ME TO SEE MY LIFE

Valerie Lee

Growing up as a Chinese American and staying in touch with my culture and tradition has been a satisfying, comforting, and fulfilling experience for me. Eating, thinking, living, and incorporating aspects of Chinese tradition into modern life is not a popular route for new generations of Chinese in this country. The benefit I've received from my studies has been priceless. Part of expanding on accumulated knowledge is to visit the roots of its existence and talk and write about your experiences. I'm preparing to visit China for the first time to do research in martial arts and Chinese medicine. Before I leave, I'm writing this essay to reflect on my thoughts and experiences in the martial arts as a Chinese American woman in America.

When I was a teenager, my kung fu class gave me a place to go where I willingly accepted discipline, which balanced out the rebellious and reckless side of my life. Although I spent days and weekends cruising around with my friends in classic Cameros, Corvettes, and Malibus, I never missed my kung fu class. Even after an all-night party I forced myself to work out. I would clomp down the studio stairs in my bell bottoms and platform shoes and be confronted by my teacher, Sifu Lai Hung. As I made a feeble attempt to brush by him to change my clothes, he would look at my eyes, pull down my lower lids, and point out my anemic

condition. Then he'd smell my hair, inspect my mouth, and accuse me of smoking cigarettes. This last accusation I could truthfully deny before managing to escape. After doing short and long forms followed by some free sparring, I'd feel recuperated from the night before, then I was ready to party again.

Sifu Lai Hung had a strong background in tournament fighting and used many techniques and training methods derived from kickboxing. My first big competition was the Singapore Southeast Asian Pugilistic Tournament. To prepare, we ran a couple of miles around the Marina Green by the San Francisco Bay, then did wind sprints in the Washington Square Park in North Beach with Sifu pacing us and bleeping on his whistle. A short walk down Columbus Avenue took us to our Chinatown studio, a concrete hole in the wall. There we jumped rope, kicked the bag, and sparred for an hour each. Then he would treat us all to lunch at the Ping Yuen Bakery and Restaurant on Grant Ave. He encouraged us to be competitive without using force against force, but somehow we still managed to bang each other up. It wasn't important whether we won or lost but that we put forth our best effort. Proper etiquette with him and fellow students was a high priority, especially after a hard punch or kick in the face.

Sifu Lai Hung, a classic kung fu movie type, often went into rages when things didn't go his way, but beyond this immature behavior existed a man dedicated to the kung fu way. He was a strict disciplinarian, often reprimanding errors in sparring and form practice with physical blows to vulnerable acupressure points. I'll always remember how he could floor me with a quick grip and press to my collarbone. After sparring with him one day, I was amazed to find his hand print bruised onto my thigh. He insisted that we always behave in the proper kung fu manner by showing loyalty to our teacher, school, and fellow students. He exemplified this code by passionately protecting and defending the honor of the school and his students without hesitation or question. He always actively participated in different phases of class with contagious enthusiasm and a variety of emotional outbursts that encouraged us to persevere and practice harder to please and appease his commanding nature. As demanding as he was with his expectations of us, he was extremely generous with physical and emotional affection, playful bantering, paternal counseling, or a free meal. The common bond I shared with my classmates provided a healthy, stable, supportive group that I could rely on. I had always been a physically active person and kung fu came to me naturally. I identified with it and enjoyed expressing myself through the movement. My practice became a way for me to focus my active teenage energy toward better concentration, endurance, stamina, and health. This was important during a time when it was not uncommon to have acquaintances arrested or shot to death in the streets.

I had studied with Sifu Lai Hung for almost six years when I decided to go to Hawaii. I had already experienced kung fu techniques on acupressure points, but I was to have an entirely different acupuncture experience when I moved to Hawaii. I found Lily Siou's School of Six Chinese Arts through the recommendation of a local Hawaiian martial artist. They practiced a soft, flowery style of *chi kung* that was very different from the combat-oriented tournament training I had been doing. At first I didn't agree with the teaching methods or style and voiced my differences to the senior students. They suggested I give the school a chance and I ended up as a live-in student at the Monastery in Aina Haina. We woke to a gong at 4:30 a.m. for our first meditation in front of a huge, elaborately decorated Daoist altar. We meditated again at 11:30 p.m. Free time was spent doing chores or *qi gong* or studying Chinese medicine. I also had a regular job as a tour guide taking tourists to Hanama Bay National Park. I was in heaven, learning Chinese medicine and martial arts in a Hawaiian paradise. My idyll ended after only one year: I returned to San Francisco because my grandmother was ill. She died after a long bout with lung cancer.

I continued my studies of Chinese medicine at San Francisco State University. Raised in a predominantly Chinese population in San Francisco North Beach-Chinatown and having lived in Hawaii, I was always part of the Asian majority. At the university, I had my first experience of being in the minority in my classes. At first I was impatient and frustrated at that situation and couldn't understand why more Asians weren't in class. White students asked questions about things that seemed second nature to me. I was bored listening to them and felt my class time was being wasted. Studying Chinese medicine is difficult because it covers so much material and requires being able to think in another cultural context. The depth and complex nature of Chinese culture makes the study of acupuncture an extremely demanding undertaking. Realizing this, I had to admire my classmates' determination to understand traditional Chinese medicine.

Learning about Chinese culture gave me a secure feeling of wholeness and understanding of myself and where my ancestors came from. It is challenging for me to constantly observe myself within the context of my own culture and to follow its traditions. I often struggled with studying Chinese culture and the dichotomy of being Chinese American and never feeling totally Chinese. Over time I resolved this conflict by learning to accept both parts of my heritage, and now I can respectfully do as my ancestors did and become responsible and educated enough to globally expand on their knowledge. This path has not always been an easy one to follow, but I've met and worked with an incredible array of people and grown to appreciate and respect all my diverse colleagues.

I travelled once more with Sifu Lai Hung, this time to compete in the Southeast Asian Pugilistic Tournament in Malaysia where I placed first by a technical knockout. Then, because of a chronic shoulder injury, I began to study Yang style Tai Chi with Sifu Fong Ha. There I met Dan Farber who eventually introduced me to my present teacher, Sifu Adam Hsu. Dan spoke of Sifu Hsu's knowledge and authenticity and showed me techniques he had learned in class. He invited me to drop by the Panhandle of Golden Gate Park to observe the class. When I finally did, in 1982, I joined immediately.

The first couple of years I focused on the Islamic Style Longfist. At that time it was the basic style that Sifu Hsu recommended because its open, expansive movements and strong stances provided a strong foundation for learning other styles. I spent the first year on *tan tuei*, ten lines of basic kicks and punches in combination. The sequence of movements was easy to learn because I had many years of experience in learning forms. But that experience became a detriment, and my instruction in the first three years of class was "to wash away my old habits." I had to clean up my movements from my previous style, or I would never capture the pure flavor of the Islamic Style Longfist. Undertaking the physical and psychological change of style was slow and difficult. I had to drop everything I had learned but maintain my self-discipline. It was hard to let go of the style that I had spent so much time and effort learning, and I didn't always see or understand how my movements were wrong with the new style.

Sifu Hsu's teaching style was completely different from what I was used to. He didn't work out with his students so that we could mimic his movements. He never showed us corrections but would explain verbally what we needed to do. He made the analogy that kung fu training was like the difference between a fast food restaurant and a fine French restaurant. I didn't always understand comparative stories, but the point he always made was that there are no short cuts in kung fu. We had to practice

36

harder and then harder again.

I remember feeling happy to learn *pao chuan*, the second level of Longfist, having something to bite into. I learned the form quickly and it gave me a sense of accomplishment. Soon I learned that with this attitude, I wouldn't last long in the class. My form at this point was like a roughly chiseled statue in need of details and features. I didn't realize I was at the beginning of a long road to refinement. The hard workouts, trying to coordinate my body, arms, and legs to do several things at once, seemed neverending. The depth of the form demands that the movements be done with athletic strength and agility while keeping the subtle details of the traditional usage intact. This element in form training is often missing and replaced with movements that are flowery, empty, and weak. With a heavy heart, Sifu would explain, "If the direction of kung fu continues with this misunderstanding, traditional martial arts will vanish and may be lost forever." As the importance of this concept became clear, the focus of my kung fu practice began to change. I've learned to look beyond my self-interest and support universal growth of Chinese culture, traditional Chinese kung fu in particular. In other words, I've lost my innocent thinking that I could practice kung fu just for the love of it. Sifu Hsu's continued passion to preserve traditional kung fu compels me to become responsible and take part to do the same.

After learning *cha chuan*, the third level of Longfist, it was evident that I didn't have the leg strength to execute the advanced Longfist techniques properly. Sifu recommended that I expand my training with Chen Tai Chi because its flavor was compatible with Longfist. My legs experienced burning sensations I never want to repeat. The long form of Chen Tai Chi has seventy-two movements. The first level of training is to hold each posture for three or more deep breaths, and the form takes 45 minutes to an hour to complete. The training process to build the endurance to practice the form this way was long, slow, and excruciating, another intense lesson that there are no short cuts in kung fu.

The slow, careful movements of Tai Chi Chuan ideally act in your body like a coil, able to contract or expand at different speeds in a spiraling motion like a spring. This method of issuing power is called "reeling silk." Having your mind and intent *(yi)* fully in the moment of Tai Chi movements develops deep concentration and focus, practical skills necessary in daily life.

This intent is especially beneficial for me because of my profession as an acupuncturist. Acupuncture needles are centimeters thin. I use this intent as I puncture through the skin and find the acupuncture point. Daily kung fu workouts strengthen me physically, balance my emotions, and calm me spiritually, which enable me to stimulate *chi*, or life force, in the body with needles in acupuncture points. These points are found by palpating along acupuncture meridians, pathways of *chi* that flow from head to toe in the body. Each of these meridians has a related internal organ. When I hold postures, I think of the meridians traveling in their respective pathways. I'm also attentive to how the tendons are reacting to different movements around my joints and which muscles are used for particular motions. Static postures use small muscles that work with and strengthen tendons around the joints.

We practice a series of eight static postures called the *ba shi*. As long as I've been in class, the *ba shi* has been the moment of truth. I could always feel the condition of my legs while holding these meditative postures. The eight stances are done on the left and right legs, coming back to and transferring from the 50-50 horse stance with the knees bent at a 90-degree angle. Deep, slow breaths are counted and focused in the *dan tien* area to cultivate and sink one's *chi*.

I used to dread the moment when we had to do the eight stances. My attitude was terribly immature and negative. I felt miserable and sorry for myself being forced into doing such a monotonous, boring, and painful exercise. Internally my biggest weaknesses of being moody and inconsistent would surface. But as much as I resisted doing the stances in my mind, I always felt better and stronger after I did them. After probably three or four years, I became stronger, was able to feel calm and relaxed, and looked forward to doing the stances as a meditation. Now I feel it's an absolute necessity to do them because it's the most effective leg training to build muscle and ligament strength and develop the proper body alignment needed for more complex movements in advanced forms. Not only has the *ba shi* helped me physically, but I've become less moody and more consistent in life.

Every time I begin a style, there is a period of adjustment to the new flavor and character. It's like meeting a new friend or lover. Sifu says, "Try any style to see if you like it, you may like it, but it may not like you, or maybe you fall in love." Each style has its own elements, like a sculpture. There's wood, clay, glass, metal, or stone sculpturing and you choose one that suits you according to your personality, taste, and natural adeptness. With kung fu you also consider physical capability and body type when choosing a style.

Bagua influenced me in a different way than Longfist or Tai Chi. The unusual extreme body twist that's required felt uncomfortable and awkward at first. I didn't really like it because the movements felt so weird. My feet, ankles, and knees felt tangled and my thighs kept getting into each other's way, which really made me feel insecure because of my thigh complex. When I thought I was twisted to the max, Sifu would say, "Turn more!" That was only the beginning standing and square walking stage. When I started walking the circle, my eyes ached because everything kept moving. When I stopped, I'd be dizzy and have a headache. My classmates thought the flexible, circular, twisting, changeable style suited my nature. Eventually the painful side effects went away, so I kept at it. Now when I practice *bagua*, I feel the twisting action massage my organs and lubricate my joints.

Bagua uses a unique curved walking step and specializes in palm and step techniques. Emphasis is on attacking from the side by applying the concept of the circle rather than confronting an opponent directly. The fighting techniques are difficult to discern in the subtle fluid movements of *bagua*, especially if it's taught incorrectly without the proper basics. The trademark of the *bagua* system is the original circling form, *ba jang* (eight palms). Often this form is the only one taught to students, which is tragic because it indicates that the system was incompletely passed on. Mystique and fantasy surrounds *bagua* because myth says immortals from heaven created *bagua*. The truth is that *bagua* is a martial art system with basics and progressive levels of training developed by Dung Hai Cuan just a hundred years ago.

Sifu Hsu often talks about having the right kung fu attitude and incorporating it into your lifestyle everyday. He also has a uniquely discriminating eye for details in kung fu movements. His depth of understanding and ability to meticulously interpret movements requires one to relentlessly strive for detail in form and take brutally honest corrections with humility and an egoless mind. The range of styles and weapons that he has mastered is so remarkable that it is hard not to be in awe of his knowledge and skill. But his manner is so unobtrusive that there is no opportunity to indulge in excessive displays of idolization. He commands that we show our appreciation by sincerely applying our best effort to learn and promote the art with the knowledge he passes on to us. "Face the truth," is a favorite quote from Sifu Adam Hsu. That's a hard virtue to follow but one that is most rewarding. My practice has become my reflection, a mirror for me to see my life. Sifu is always pushing his students to stretch to find the truth and face a clear and honest picture of themselves.

San Francisco is a melting pot of cultures and the kung fu capital of America. I live a block away from the Panhandle of Golden Gate Park, a haven for martial artists. For years I've stepped out my front door into the spacious park filled with eucalyptus trees to sweat away my anxieties, fears, doubts, and troubles. As a native of this tolerant city, one could say I've lived a sheltered existence where I can be secure and accepted. Now, I'm packing my bags to embark on a lengthy tour of China, where I'll think, eat, and speak as an American and only hope to pass as a Chinese and uncover deeper truths about traditional Chinese culture.

OPEN TO CHANGE: STEPS ALONG THE WAY

Kathy Hopwood

It was an amazing process for me to go beyond who "I should have been" to who I am now. I should have been dependent on welfare, living in public housing, beaten and battered, addicted to drugs or dead from an overdose. Instead I am alive, creative, proud, self-educated, and a self-employed business woman.

I was born in Washington, DC into a poor and uneducated family. My father grew up in a part of DC where there were still woods to hunt and fish in. My mother grew up on a nearby farm that was rapidly becoming urbanized. I remember my parents, two scared and very young adults, raising a family when they were barely out of their teens.

We lived in subsidized public housing in the Southeastern section of DC. Living in public housing meant that a family of eight people was cramped into a small box house that gave no privacy. My family survived by periodically going on welfare when my father was unable to find work. My father was a "Jack of All Trades and Master of None." He held jobs as a police guard, cab driver, housepainter, tile-setter—but mostly he was an extremely frustrated artist. When the complexities of life got to him, he drank. He drank everyday. With the alcoholism came battering and neglect. As a link in the chain of family violence, he passed on the abuse he had experienced growing up. My mother had total

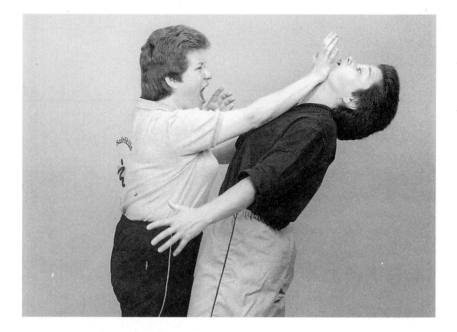

responsibility for rearing the children and little knowledge of how to do this. She had married to escape her own abusive family. My mother developed the "learned helplessness syndrome" often associated with battered wives. She had no self-esteem, no education, and no options for change; consequently, she was depressed and often suicidal.

This was in the early 50's and 60's, the days before battered women's shelters existed. People did not talk about such things, battering was considered a private family matter. A man's house was his castle and the family was expected to take the abuse. Our daily problems were a constant battle of figuring out how to get food and clothing, avoiding abuse, and trying to develop some sense of sanity. My task was to grow up in one piece in this hopeless situation.

I dropped out of school and left home at fifteen, roaming the streets of DC, trying to figure myself out. Many other teens had "taken to the streets" in hopes of making changes in the world or, like me, simply trying to escape a difficult family situation. The drugs and street climate were very tough but not as deadly as now. It was the era of Vietnam war protests, love-ins, peace gatherings, and other hippie phenomenon. We considered ourselves revolutionaries working toward a new world. Make no mistake about the climate for women though, sexual harassment and rape definitely were a part of that culture—we just didn't have a name for them yet.

Having no real direction in my life, I just floated along. At such a tender age, I had no education, no self-esteem, and no aspirations. I experienced many sexual assault attempts by both strangers on the street and guys I knew and trusted. I often wondered if I had giant bull's-eye on me saying "Here's a perfect target." Fortunately, I was not raped but I too often just escaped from assault situations by the skin of my teeth. It seemed as though I was constantly negotiating for the rights of my body.

At the time, I looked at this phenomenon from a totally personal perspective, thinking that it was something about me, some way I walked or perhaps the clothes I wore. The fact that I was female, alone, hanging out on the streets, and from the lower end of the socioeconomic scale didn't cross my mind as contributing factors. Eventually I came to understand that I was harassed and attacked simply because I was female. This was a stunning revelation to have to live with, and I didn't like it one bit.

I heard about a karate class for women starting through the newly formed Women's Center. Women were just beginning to organize around the issue of rape, and martial arts training certainly made sense. Although I had no idea what I was getting myself into, the thought of being able to stomp on my next attacker appealed to my usually non-violent, peace-loving self.

On arriving at my first karate class, I discovered several startling truths. The instructor expected us to work hard at this stuff! Not only that, she wanted us to take ourselves seriously! There was to be no talking, smiling, or playing around, which was difficult because most of the women had attended the class with groups of friends and we were all goofing around to ease our nervousness. Furthermore, students were supposed to line up in neat lines and follow her directions. Shades of gym class! What was this? The military or something? I was beginning to think that this weird stuff was not for me. Besides, I couldn't make a proper fist or get my feet into those awkward positions she wanted us to do for a side kick! In fact I couldn't stretch, or bend, or get my knee up, or breathe, or most of all, not feel ridiculously silly. At the first opportunity, I escaped to the bathroom and cried for a long time. I considered myself pretty tough from the years on the streets. Yet here I was crying my eyes out because my tough self-image had finally collided with my very real and very fragile self-esteem of being a survivor. This collision would change the course of my life forever.

That was in 1972 and fortunately, I hung in there. Now I can do all those "ridiculously silly" things that teacher wanted me to do. It has taken hard work and years of commitment but I believe the hardest step was not hiding from the emotional challenge that took place in that first class. Martial arts training holds the opportunity for one to face oneself honestly and with self-love, to create real changes in oneself and in the world.

Martial arts training helped me to become more than just a survivor of a negligent and harsh upbringing. I became someone who could create choice in her life. This transition required that I honestly recognize my strengths and weakness. The next step was to take real care of myself, to become loving of myself, to gain the skills that would enable me to defend myself when necessary. I came to understand that I did not have to let anyone harm me with either physical or verbal assaults. Now all I have to do is continue taking steps along the path that I not only "collided" with but have actively chosen as my life's work.

Perhaps the biggest lesson I learned from my involvement in the martial arts is to be open to those golden opportunities of change. Martial arts training forced me to challenge myself and change who I was and who I was supposed to become. A high level of belief in myself has resulted from these changes. Call it self-esteem, self-respect, or self-pride but it stems from the core of the self. This belief has helped me found a *dojo*, the Triangle Women's Martial Arts Center, and to create a business, SafeSkills Associates. Through both endeavors, I am able to offer the training that has been so valuable to me in my life changes.

It has been an amazing process for me to undergo my own changes, and now I am privileged to participate in other women's process of self-discovery. Teaching women to make a fist, kick a target, or let out a ferocious animal yell for the first time is an honor that I will treasure for the rest of my steps along the way.

TO STRETCH AND FLY

Ellie Doermann

I practice my horse stance and I try to make muscles and bones do things I never believed they could do. I struggle to sink low and sit straight, to distribute my weight so that I am immovable yet ready to move in an instant. I am frustrated that my knee aches sometimes, reminder of an old injury, and that I frequently pull the muscles in my right hip. It helps to remember the times when I could hardly walk after a class of horse stances, when my legs quivered and wanted to collapse if I did not lock my knees. I felt the exact aching definition of every muscle for several days afterward and pulled myself up the back stairs because my legs did not want to lift me. I cried at home because I did not know if I could continue, and I knew that if I gave up, I would be giving up on myself. I now know that I am not giving up, and that makes it all a little easier.

As I sit in horse stance my right foot still turns out and I lean forward. I have landed on my butt more often than I can count. Some days I am convinced my body will stretch no further. I only rarely feel like I sit in a place of power and draw energy up from the earth; the feeling comes in fleeting glimpses. As I get closer to horse stance, I strain and ache. Some days my pelvis feels locked, my hips refuse my efforts to sink and connect, as if to say, "Who do you think you are, to want to be a boxer?"

I have been up against some powerful lessons my body learned a long time ago. Training has helped me to move the rage, pain, and helplessness that were locked up and hidden silently away for so long. Memories of sexual abuse hidden from conscious view drove me to learn to fight in the first place. I could not explain it at first, but I sensed my emotional and spiritual survival depended on defending myself, claiming my space and my experience. My training helped me create and defend the space to face myself.

As memories had room to return they became precious to me and guided my training. I sometimes felt they were the one thing no one could take from me. As I learned to spar the old feelings and images were right in front of me. Fighting was a serious matter. I learned to fight with tears streaming down my face when pushed to that point of fatigue when the usual masks do not hold up any more. Then I learned to call up anger from a deep well in my gut to provide me the energy to keep going when I wanted to stop. This anger seemed to work, but as time went on, I started feeling drained. Physical recovery took longer. I knew I had to find another source of power to move me, one that did not deplete me.

Fighting is no longer so heavy a matter, though it demands more of everything I have. I fight for the satisfaction of accomplishment, and the more I smile inside the more powerfully I move. I still cry often enough but the tears are no longer of grief for an injured child. Rather they are tears of frustration as I continue to run up against myself, frustration that I cannot get from where I am to where I want to be, frustration that I cannot be patient with myself. I want to fly with the wind! But I cannot fly while carrying the weight of all that is past. To commit myself fully to this moment means I must forgive and let go, hard to imagine when I have devoted so much of my adult life to unravelling the past and holding on tight. This must be the hardest training yet.

The transition from defining and embracing my experience and my boundaries to releasing them and moving with Spirit is not always clear to me. I have no road map and I must go on

faith. My teacher has said that we are powerless against the force of a tornado or tidal wave, but if we choose to move with that energy we become unstoppable. I must learn to trust that I am safe moving with a force far greater than I and to realize that the danger lies in hesitation. I must be right here right now because if my mind wanders to last night or tomorrow I can get hurt. The ancient motions draw me back to my body, which as a victim I learned to leave behind, keeping me centered and safe.

Old voices still try to tell me I cannot. I can't do a horse stance, I can't jump, I can't balance, I can't kick. I have lots of good arguments: I will hurt myself, I will hurt my partner, or on a deeper level, I will betray the lesson that I must remain powerless.

Now I train for those magic moments when everything comes together and works. Those moments seem few but are worth waiting for and working for. Some days I plug away and there is no inspiration in it. I go through my practiced moves, but I have sandbags for feet and steel bands for muscles. I cannot hold a stance or get a leg up to kick. When I shut myself off from Source, from Spirit, there is no breath of magic. My body is limited, but with a breath of inspiration anything seems possible. Possibility keeps me going. Those moments only happen when I can empty myself of the old anger. The desire to prove something to someone stops the magic. When I imagine getting back at someone for all they have done, my strikes become stiff and I throw myself off balance. The kind of rage that was once so useful does not work any more.

Part of training is to learn to move through obstacles as if they do not exist, rather than to engage with them and change to fit them. I find my most persistent opponents are inside myself. I can accommodate myself to them, or I can decide to move through them to whatever lies on the other side. I do not know what is there but I know that I must forgive the past to get there. I know I have to let go and free my body and my spirit to stretch and fly.

SURVIVING
A MURDER

Deborah Wheeler

Five years ago my mother was raped and beaten to death by a teenaged neighbor. I would like to share with you how my martial arts training helped me survive.

I have been a martial artist for almost twenty years, although I didn't always see myself that way. I started studying T'ai Chi Ch'uan at the suggestion of my calligraphy teacher. I was a pacifist and utterly opposed to the idea of fighting, so every time we discussed the applications of the graceful, meditative movements, I wouldn't listen. Gradually I came to realize that, no matter what my political ideals, there was a side of me that was aggressive, even violent. More than that, this side would not simply go away because I refused to deal with it. What it would do was go underground, subconscious and ready to explode.

About this time, a woman friend who studied Kung Fu San Soo took me to her school. San Soo is an ancient Chinese fighting style, circular yet vigorous, encompassing a wide variety of techniques. It looked to me like a barroom brawl—people, men mostly, kicking and punching and throwing each other all over the mat. I was so upset at the sight, I decided to confront my feelings by getting out on the mat myself.

At first I thought my years of T'ai Chi Ch'uan would give me an advantage, but the first time my partner aimed a fist at my

nose, all my philosophy went out the window. I became a beginner, an egg. Through two pregnancies and innumerable bruises and sprains over sixteen years I kept training. I learned to trust my partners and I learned to trust myself, even that hidden, violent part of me. It was like learning to ride a tiger, requiring total concentration and clarity. I realized how much less violent I became when my energies came into balance.

Then on a gray September afternoon, a phone call came from my sister, telling me our mother had died. Not until I had flown to the city where she'd lived, along with my husband and infant daughter, did I learn of the brutal murder. Within a week, the suspect, who later pled guilty, was in custody.

At first I was so overwhelmed by shock and grief it was all I could do to exist from moment to moment. One of the most urgent things I had to do was tell my seven-year-old daughter, who arrived a few days later with her "second mommy," the same friend who had introduced me to kung fu. I called the local victim witness counselor for help, but more importantly, I drew on the focus and concentration I'd learned over years of training. I had to tell my daughter the truth, both factually and emotionally. I had to use my yang energies, instead of hiding from them.

The second important thing I had to do was deal with the unbelievable rage I felt. I was flooded by waking nightmares of what I would do to the killer if I were ever in the same room with him. I envisioned the exact techniques I'd use on him, and I would shake with fury. When I spoke at the funeral, I said, "I could kill the bastard who did this!" And I meant it. Literally.

I went home with my family, I found a counselor through the local crime victim center, and I began the long, slow process of surviving. I went back to the kung fu studio full of doubts. My mother's killer was a man, and so were most of my partners. What if I flipped out into a killing rage? Yet in the studio I felt surrounded by love and support. Many of these men were cops, veterans, and ex-gang members. One of them told me, in all seriousness, "Say the word and we'll make sure he's taken out." For me this was a real test, and it frightened the living daylights out of me. Again I rode the tiger, using my strength and balance to reaffirm my principles of respect for human life. I was answerable to my own conscience, not to the fury of the moment. I had not trained to become a killer, not even a remote, passive killer.

I began to work out again. At first my concentration was patchy, and I'd lost a lot of conditioning during my pregnancy. I was careful to pick partners who didn't resemble the killer and who were experienced enough to take care of both of us if my focus slipped. As my timing and self-confidence returned, I started putting more emotional content into my techniques. I knew this was a safe place and that nothing would happen that I didn't intend. The more I let my feelings out, the less focused on them I became. As soon as I stepped out onto the mat, I entered a new, clear space. Everything else got left behind. My moves took on a new power and decisiveness.

After a while I thought I was doing pretty well. A brown belt asked me to spar with him. He was young and slender, like the killer, but I thought I was past the point of confusion. I worked out with him until he backed off, looking very frightened. I couldn't understand why until my friend told me I'd wiped him all over the mat and "intimidated the hell" out of him. After that, I decided to give myself more time to recover.

As a surviving family member, I was legally entitled to speak at the sentencing of my mother's killer. As I wrote and rewrote my speech, I visualized the courtroom—the judge, the attorneys . . . and the killer. I was no less outraged and furious at him than a few months ago, but I knew my anger would serve me. I would use my words as a weapon, just as I might use my fists or feet. Just as I had learned to transform my pacifist ideals into a new balance, now I stripped away layers of polite usage and caution. I spoke to the parole board years in the future. I spoke to the community and my family. I spoke for a woman who no longer had a voice, and in a way, for all women. And when my mother's killer hid his face and cried, the power that spoke through me did not waver.

The ordeal is not over. Sean DeRutte, the murderer of my mother, Jane Ross, has been moved from high-security Folsom Prison to the California Men's Colony at San Luis Obispo. In a few years he will be eligible for parole. Until that day I will keep training in mind, body, and spirit.

OPPRESSION
AND A WARRIOR'S WAY

Maria Doest

Racism and sexism have caused some people to try to close the doors that stood before me in the martial arts. Rather than describe some of those situations, I'd like to point out the value of struggle. What I know is that struggle is a great teacher. And I know that I am who I am thanks to the lessons of my struggles and my heritage.

Since childhood I have felt drawn to the martial arts. Due to my American Indian and Chinese racial memory, I have been able to understand the philosophy and spirituality of the martial arts without having to learn the hard way. Karate feels like a way to go back to the source, and those were the feelings I had when I was in China and Japan. In China I felt profoundly connected, and I felt as if I had been there before. In Okinawa and Japan I felt the ancientness of my art and the preciousness of the gift of my physical, mental, and spiritual training.

Many women find the rigidity of formal martial arts training negative and male. Some women rebel while others imitate men. I believe my Native side understands and cherishes the value of being a trusting and obedient student. This ability allows a teacher to guide and nourish a student. And it allows a student to become a teacher in the same way and continue the cycle of knowledge.

I stayed with my first instructor, who was unkind, to gain his

knowledge. Sometimes I joke about not being smart enough to know I could leave! But in staying, I gained tremendous knowledge from him. It's important to take knowledge where you find it rather than close your mind. We can throw out the oppressive nonsense and keep the rest. But, and this is the tricky part when you have a minimum of knowledge, it is not always easy to tell what is oppressive and what is a lesson.

I'm afraid that the white American way is usually a "show me" attitude that approaches knowledge in a challenging, skeptical, and negative way. This is where my inborn spiritual knowledge has helped me. While my brown skin has resulted in occasions of hurtful behavior by others, it has given me many positives. I understand by saying that I risk romanticizing my position as a woman of color, but my purpose is not to be politically correct. My purpose is to share my experiences as a woman of color in the martial arts, and I believe the positive always outweighs the negative.

At the risk of sounding clichéd, if I am in a negative situation, I make it positive by changing it, by learning from it, or by removing myself from it. This way of living comes not from a specific familial example, but from my racial memory, a memory that is overwhelmingly positive while being realistic about oppression and genocide. If you focus on the negative it will eat you up and your oppressors will win. Positive energy, calm, laughing in the face of adversity, and light spiritedness—these are the ways of the warrior, the do in karate-do.

I have struggled with so many challenges in my life. I struggle with racism, sexism, disability, and more. And most importantly, I struggle with myself. I am here for a reason. I was given this physical form for a reason. My struggles and experiences have made me who I am.

FROM FATSO TO BREAKFALLS: LEARNING TO ACCEPT MY BODY

Carol A. Wiley

In the seventh grade I sat and watched the teacher weigh and measure the height of the other students, then send them out to recess. I stepped on the scale: 5'7" and 214 pounds. The teacher had not wanted to embarrass me in front of the other children, yet her disapproval was obvious. All my life I had heard from adults that I should lose weight. All my life I had endured the taunts of other children: "Fatso." "Titanic." Two more years of this pressure and, at fourteen, I began fifteen years of yo-yo dieting and trying to fit my body into a package deemed acceptable by society.

I lost fifty pounds when I was fourteen, which met with everyone's approval, but I was a shy teenager, uncomfortable with people, and losing weight didn't give me the popularity I wanted. Yet out of this loneliness grew an interest that has become central to the development of both my body and my mind. Movies and books were my companions. I saw nearly every appropriately rated movie that showed at the one theater in town, which included many of the Bruce Lee and other kung fu movies popular in the early 1970s. The movement I saw on the screen fascinated me, and I longed to try it for myself.

No one taught the marital arts in my small town, so I enrolled in a kung fu class in a nearby city, but getting to class was difficult and I dropped it after about two weeks. I attempted a karate class

during my first year of college. That also lasted about two weeks. In both classes I was reticent and self-conscious, and the instructors did nothing to encourage me, they even seemed amused I was there: I was a woman, I was big, I was uncoordinated.

But my desire to study the martial arts didn't disappear. During my senior year of college, 1979, I started a karate class and stuck with it. Although still self-conscious, I felt less out of place in this physical education class where I blended in with about twenty-five other uncoordinated people. I learned techniques as well as anyone else, sometimes better, and I was soon hooked.

I finished college, moved to a new city, and found a Tae Kwon Do class. I started the class with ten other people; after a year I was the only one still training; after two and a half years I was the senior student; after three and a half years I received my black belt. My coordination and strength improved tremendously, as did my concentration and focus. Yet I still fought my body: During that time I weighed 180–190 pounds and was constantly berating myself and trying to lose weight.

A few months after receiving my black belt I moved to another city and returned to school for a master's degree. I trained at the university Tae Kwon Do club for three months, but didn't like the instructor's approach. To try something different, I trained in Arnis (Filipino stick-fighting) for six months, but then that was no longer available. For sixteen months I did not train. I kept putting it off. I had gained about forty pounds. I thought this weight would prevent me from training the way I used to, and I was embarrassed to go into a school and say I had a black belt. But my desire to train was greater than my doubts, and I started training again in Tae Kwon Do in 1986.

I didn't lose weight, which surprised and bothered me at first, but as I saw my body respond to the physical activity, I thought less about my weight. Because the Tae Kwon Do school had only been open a few months, I soon became the senior student and assistant instructor. In 1988 I received my second degree black belt.

When the Tae Kwon Do school closed in 1989, I decided to expand my martial arts experience and began training in Aikido. My proficiency with the linear movements of Tae Kwon Do did not translate immediately to the circular and spiral movements of Aikido. I also had to learn to fall and roll, which was a frustrating and sometimes painful experience. Aikido classes did not give me the exhilarated feeling that Tae Kwon Do classes usually had. More often I felt depressed and frustrated.

The difficult transition almost led me to quit Aikido and find a Tae Kwon Do school. I wasn't sure why I stuck with Aikido, but somehow I felt there was something to learn. After a year I enjoyed the movement of Aikido, felt less awkward, and had begun to understand Aikido's approach. Then came a big moment: I did my first breakfall. A breakfall is like a half-flip, a roll without any contact with the mat. I never thought my body could fly through the air like that.

The physical benefits of the martial arts are obvious: Improved coordination, strength, and endurance. But the mental benefits are more important: The true martial artist knows that the mind is a more powerful weapon than the body. Training develops focus, concentration, awareness, and self-confidence. These elements are important not only in a self-defense situation but also in all other areas of life.

When people ask why I train in the martial arts, I often say that I train for the satisfaction of doing something physically useful and mentally challenging. But deep inside I know that I cannot not train, for training fills an important part of my being. When things are right, it's pure pleasure. Of course, there's also the exhaustion and occasional injury. And sometimes nothing seems to work, and it's pure frustration. Through it all I feel something deep in my being that I know is more important than the momentary pleasure or pain.

The martial arts have been important in helping me accept my body. If I can do all this, what's so great about being thin? A few years ago I stopped dieting, tentatively at first, but with increasing conviction, especially as I read more about the dangers of yo-yo dieting. I eat nutritiously and let my weight find its own level, a level that has proven to be neither the lightest nor heaviest I have been as an adult. Weight is now a much less important part of my life, but the martial arts remain important, training my body, my mind, and my spirit.

MARTIAL ARTS OUT OF A WHEELCHAIR: A POSSIBILITY OR NOT?

Lydia Zijdel

Yes, martial arts out of a wheelchair are possible. Therefore, this story is about me—Lydia Zijdel, a Karateka and Aikidoka, forty-one years old, practicing karate and Aikido out of a wheelchair—and about the approximately 250 other disabled people to whom I have taught self-defense over the past five and a half years.

It all started in November 1984 when I went to a self-defense weekend for women in wheelchairs or on crutches who had good arm function. This course was the first of its kind ever to be held in Europe. The two teachers, Inge Ruys and Sybilla Claus, are able-bodied self-defense teachers with much experience in the field of self-defense for women and in the martial arts. They felt these courses should also be open to disabled women. During that weekend I came together with a group of very interesting women, all curious about what self-defense could bring to women with disabilities. I don't know what happened to me, but I fell in love with this kind of using (or should I say reusing) of my body, and I started to fight back. Not only did I learn some techniques to defend myself, but I also started to love my disabled body again. I saw what she was still capable of doing, instead of seeing what she could not do anymore.

After this course I started to read about the martial arts and to phone local self-defense schools for more courses, this time

with able-bodied women only. From reading I became more and more interested in Aikido, a martial art that does not focus on body strength in the first place but more on internal *ki* and circular body movement. I desperately looked for an Aikido school because of my disappointment in training with self-defense teachers who had hardly any experience teaching women with disabilities and who had never gone to the trouble Inge and Sybilla had to teach such a group of women. But my disappointment became even bigger. If there was in the self-defense movement hardly any thought for this group of women, in the martial arts world it was even worse. Phoning and writing to different Aikido schools taught me how many martial artists think about martial arts for disabled people. Some said I was really crazy, others that their schools were not accessible, others that it was absolutely impossible to train in Aikido out of a wheelchair.

Then, on a Sunday evening in February 1985, at a moment I had nearly given up hope, I received a phone call from Erik Louw, Sensei (4th Dan Aikido, 4th Dan Kenjutsu). His first words were, "Hi, I am Erik, I have never taught people with disabilities before, my school is not accessible at all, but I would love to teach you!" I was speechless. That Wednesday I met him in an accessible pub, not far from his *dojo,* and he talked about Aikido and about his life. I immediately grew very fond of this small and warmhearted guy.

After five cups of coffee and the arrival of one of Erik's students, we went to his *dojo,* a small *dojo* in one of the many canal houses in Amsterdam. A large staircase went down. Erik and his student carried me down the stairs, and the first class started. At that time I was not even able to sit up straight in my wheelchair, I had no balance whatsoever, and I had a hard time moving myself out of the wheelchair. Erik has been teaching me ever since, one private class a week and two other classes with the other students. After a few months I could sit on my own on the floor. Now I hold the rank of nikkyu in Aikido, and I can sit for hours on the floor and do more than sit!

Since October 1990 we have taught a special class for people with disabilities. Erik Sensei is a wonderful teacher who never uses the words, "This is not possible for you." He adapts the techniques but keeps the principle of Aikido as it was meant by O'Sensei. Erik introduced me to his teacher, Kanetsuka Sensei, a Japanese teacher living in England, and he asked Kanetsuka Sensei to test me regularly for my ranks, as he is the most strict teacher. Erik never wanted me to have the feeling that I would get my ranks just because I am disabled, although he acknowledged the extra effort you have to put in as a disabled person.

In July 1985 the annual Feminist International Summer Training (FIST '85) was to be held again in the Netherlands. I did not have enough hours to apply, but since my business and private partner was going and had told me so much about these camps and their importance for martial arts women, I decided to apply anyhow. The organization was not stupid at a time when training with a disability was becoming a big topic, and although I did not have enough hours, they allowed me to come to camp and "used me" for their publicity. It was a great camp. I may have lacked the necessary hours, but I noticed that the few months of training with Erik Sensei had given me more experience than some of the women in the Aikido class with the required hours.

I went to a variety of classes. Some teachers knew what to do with me, how to adapt their classes—they all knew beforehand that a woman in a wheelchair with good arm function was coming—but in other classes I was completely ignored. (The same would happen to me one year later at Special Training.[1]) At FIST I met Wendi Dragonfire Sensei (4th Dan Shuri Ryu Karate, 2nd Dan Modern Arnis) and I attended all her street and stick fighting classes. She invited me to the classes that she would start in the Netherlands. In September 1985 I became her student and friend, and in December of that same year I realized that what had started as stick and street fighting classes turned out to be karate. I stayed, and I hold the rank of first degree black belt in Shuri Ryu Karate.

Training in one martial art as a disabled person is hard, but training in two different styles is crazy. But I was, and still am, possessed by the martial arts. They are my life. Not only training itself but also using everything I have learned to teach the self-defense courses I have been giving since 1985 to women and men with disabilities. It all started in 1984 with that course for women in wheelchairs or on crutches who had good arm function. Now the courses have grown to include women with all kinds of disabilities: spastic women, small women, women with hardly any strength or movement. The goal in these courses is always that there is a possibility for everyone to learn how to defend oneself. I have taught over 250 women, girls, men, and boys in many different countries in Europe. I also started Teachers Training Courses for self-defense and martial arts teachers who are interested in making their courses or schools more open to people with disabilities. The experience I have gathered in teaching over the years will definitely be used in the book I am writing about the subject.

Besides teaching self-defense and martial arts to other disabled women and men, I also teach karate and self-defense to

---

[1]Special Training is an annual martial arts training camp for women in the United States.

mostly able-bodied girls and women. In September 1991 I started a Shuri Ryu Karate School in the center of the Netherlands. Teaching women and girls how to kick is very challenging if you cannot kick. But a lot of creativity from my side, the patience of my teachers, and the love and understanding from my karate students makes it possible.

Too often I missed examples, teachers who are disabled like I am, or other disabled women who stayed to train longer than just a few months (most of the time they could not cope with the speed of the able-bodied women), women who could understand the suffering you have to go through to learn and train in the martial arts. After every illness, even the smallest cold or setback, I had to regain my physical and mental strength more than an able-bodied person. Also, going to the *dojo* means getting in the car, getting two wheelchairs and my gear and *gi* in, driving in traffic jams after a hard day's work (I work as a Social and Educational Trainer), using my arms for every move I make. Then the hours of actual training mean my arms do not get to rest either. It's not the easiest way, but so far it's the most rewarding, especially because of the many disabled people who have started martial arts or self-defense after seeing me do it.

Special Training 1989 was especially open to women with disabilities, and I am still very sorry I was not invited to share my skills with American women. The USA has a lot of experience in martial arts, and perhaps also in martial arts and self-defense for women with disabilities. But in Europe we have also gathered much experience, and teaching more than 250 disabled people in six years has given me a lot of experience that cannot be taught within a ranking system.

I hope that the Special Trainings in the future and any other martial arts events will stay or be open again to women with disabilities, and one day I hope to be invited to teach at one. The martial arts do not necessarily have to stop if you become injured or disabled. The mental and physical wounds have to heal to a certain extent, but after this healing, open your heart again for your martial art.

MARTIAL ARTS
AND WOMEN'S SELF-DEFENSE:
TWO PERSPECTIVES

Debbie Leung

Before I begin a self-defense workshop for women, someone usually asks me, "Are you going to teach us some karate?" Both the general public and many martial artists equate self-defense with the martial arts. I have been a martial artist since 1978 and an instructor of self-defense for women since 1980. These two pursuits have led me down separate paths that do not cross as often as one would think.

My first exposure to these worlds of martial art and self-defense was in a women's karate class in 1978. Not knowing what to expect, I tagged along with several co-workers. I went partly out of curiosity and partly for adventure. Looking back, I realize that something deep in my being must have also drawn me to that first class because, after thirteen years, I continue to participate in the martial arts and in the movement to end assaults against women.

My involvement with martial arts practice, now centered on kung fu, and women's self-defense evolved into separate commitments, both important parts of who I am while playing different roles in my life. Women's self-defense is a practical response to the violence women face. After working in rape crisis centers and battered women's shelters and listening to women in self-defense classes describe the violence they have faced, I and the group of self-defense teachers I work with have found that much

of the violence can be best addressed in ways other than with martial arts fighting skills. Many self-defense programs for women primarily address the fighting aspects, which many women may not feel appropriate for much of the violence they encounter.

Martial arts practice plays different roles for different people. For me, it has been a road with many twists, turns, and forks. The more I travel along this road, the more I learn about myself. It has addressed issues of body, emotion, mind, spirit, and culture. Martial arts practice positively affects my approach to life in general while training me to win the ultimate fight, one with an opponent who tests me physically and mentally past the limits. Although I think many women in self-defense classes could benefit from these lessons, I cannot expect all women who have a practical immediate need for self-defense information to make the personal commitment needed to get these benefits from a martial art. I feel that my martial arts practice has made me a better self-defense teacher because it has given me a broader perspective of the possibilities of what women can do, not just physically but also in other realms.

A Women's Definition of Self-Defense

What is important to women learning self-defense has become increasingly clear as I continue to teach, listen to survivors of violence, and work with other women working to end violence against women. In 1979 several members of my first karate class started FIST (Feminists in Self-Defense Training in Olympia, Washington) because we wanted greater freedom to develop programs accessible to larger numbers of women. The foundation and content of FIST's programs are not based in a martial art.

The link with martial arts makes learning "self-defense" a dubious option for many women. Fears about hurting and injuring others, even attackers, and about being unable to keep up physically are common. Participating in strenuous physical activity after a lifetime of not being athletic can be intimidating, especially for women who were taught that it is "unladylike." The time and economic commitment are large. In addition, the issue of "self-defense" relates so closely to abuse and assault that thinking, talking, and doing something about it can feel especially frightening and risky in a male-dominated activity such as the martial arts.

Some women, including me, took a big step and learned self-defense in martial arts schools. Although our lives are greatly enriched by practicing a martial art, we felt a need to share our skills in a more practical manner that can reach larger numbers of women. After years of training, talking to each other, and working in agencies supporting victims of sexual assault and domestic violence, some of us began to think about self-defense for women in a new way.

Our new concept of self-defense was influenced by the women in our communities who confronted and survived violence. We found that, contrary to many people's images of assault against women where a backfist to the nose or kick to the groin can be indisputably appropriate, most women are assaulted by men they are acquainted with and perhaps know quite well. The assaults often begin with casual conversation in a safe, public place where assailants attempt to test their dominance.[1] Stopping the assault here is usually a preferred tactic rather than waiting for physical violence to begin. It is usually easy to diffuse an assault successfully at this stage when women listen to their intuition and are willing to risk embarrassment, possibly being wrong, or overreacting.

Assaults committed by men known to women include domestic abuse, both emotional and physical, and sexual harassment and assault, which include sexist jokes, name-calling, unwanted touch, threats, rape, and incest. A study of women who were raped or experienced attempted rape found that 89% were assaulted by someone they knew.[2] One third of the assailants were dates, boyfriends, lovers, ex-lovers, husbands, or ex-husbands.

In addition, many women experience violence based on their race, ability, age, and sexual preference. As women and members of groups sharing these and other characteristics, we are all at risk of assault because many people generally consider us vulnerable, weak, and/or passive. Men who assault us are not usually looking for a fight, but want an easy situation in which to overpower, control, or dominate another person.[3] These experiences with abuse and assault, together with our experiences learning to defend ourselves, have evolved into a new definition of "self-defense," a women's definition.

Self-defense is a way of nurturing ourselves by caring about our own safety and the safety of others. It involves intuition and making choices. We can use self-defense to create a safe, supportive, and caring environment. Self-defense skills and strategies are much more than methods for defending against attackers. These skills and strategies have many uses and help improve the overall quality of everyday life for women. Most importantly, when used in situations not potentially threatening, these skills

---

[1]"Queens Bench Foundation Study, Part III, Conclusions," Law Enforcement Assistance Association (LEAA), 1976.

[2]*Sexual Exploitation: Rape, Child Sexual Abuse, and Workplace Harassment*, Diana Russell, Sage Publications, 1984.

[3]"Queens Bench Foundation Study, Part III, Conclusions," LEAA, 1976

enhance our ability as women to cultivate our awareness of ourselves, our relationships with others, and our enjoyment of the world. These skills help us, including those with limited physical ability, have more control over and improve our lives. Regularly using these self-defense skills and strategies in non-threatening situations lets us recall and apply the skills readily when our safety is threatened.

This concept of self-defense emphasizes prevention, avoidance, deterrence, and survival strategies. Techniques for escaping from an assailant are included but the primary goal is to eliminate the need for escape tactics and techniques. FIST's programs stress the need for the following important elements of self-defense that we can incorporate into our daily lives:

- accurate information about assaults common to women as the primary aspect of prevention,
- awareness of the environment around us by using our physical and intuitive senses to avoid dangerous or uncomfortable encounters before they begin,
- skills for appearing confident and assertive to deter assault when an assailant begins dominating or controlling a situation, and
- survival mechanisms for maintaining our dignity and self-esteem in difficult situations.

FIST was founded on the belief that women of all ages, sizes, physical abilities, and cultural and economic backgrounds have the right and ability to defend themselves successfully. FIST's programs differ from most self-defense programs by being based on women's experience with violence, with learning self-defense, and with resisting assault successfully. These programs empower women to trust their instincts and use their abilities.

One Woman's Perspective on the Martial Arts

As I settle down to think and write about the martial arts, my feelings are not as clear as they are regarding self-defense for women. The feelings float in and out of consciousness, unable to emerge into words. My feelings are difficult to grasp because the martial arts play an important part in my personal growth and in defining what it means to me to be human.

While sitting in horse stance in what seems like forever or repeating a technique over and over in search of perfection, tears want to burst forth from the pain and frustration. But something in me says, "Don't give up. There's a lesson in this." Then, when I least think it will happen, my head clears, the stance feels strong, the technique flies, it is powerful, and it feels natural. It is a glimpse of what my teacher calls spirit, a oneness with nature that the proper practice of the martial arts can bring.

My practice is one that calls on tradition. This means there is a correct way to execute motions in every minute detail, which the ancestors perfected to embody the power, quickness, and suppleness demonstrated in nature. We must work toward achieving that perfection so that we can learn and pass on the same art that has endured the test of time. By becoming a formidable warrior, a person who executes techniques with perfection and spirit also grows in her oneness with nature.

This kind of training also means learning the traditional names of techniques, understanding history, and practicing the rituals. By doing so, we are given a gift, an art created by my ancestors. If we can merge with the art, we can then pass it on and keep the tradition alive. It is a connection to my past, my culture.

In martial arts, fighting is the medium from which other lessons are learned. I learn how the body, spirit, and mind interrelate. The mind, the part of us which many believe makes us distinctly human, often hinders this quest to achieve the art. Fear, trust, ego, and mental dependencies are issues that get in the way. To continue to learn the art, I must deal head-on with these issues. I learn about my humanness while at the same time I try to work past it.

One can also learn about self-defense. Deducing the practical skills useful in real life situations, however, is often left to the student since most martial arts are steeped in history, tradition, culture, and sport. Self-defense skills learned through a martial art usually focus on the mental and physical aspects of fighting. Preparation and skills are not usually taught for dealing with violence at the hands of acquaintances, identifying an assault before it escalates into violence, avoiding potentially threatening encounters, being verbally assertive, and using other non-fighting options to escape assault. Two other important components to a self-defense program for women are not usually provided in martial arts schools: accurate information about violence against women to destroy the many myths that exist about it and examples of the many instances of success women have had in diffusing and escaping assault.

Women's Self-Defense and Martial Art

My martial art practice shows me that, among other things, women can become empowered emotionally, spiritually, and physically to fight back successfully against the violence we face. Women's self-defense is a factual, practical, and supportive program geared specifically to the dynamics and realities surrounding violence against women. Fighting is a last result, one option among many. Women who participate in FIST's self-defense programs usually leave them beaming from a new sense of empowerment. Like yin and yang, the roots of nature in the Chinese philosophy that pervades the Chinese martial arts, martial arts and women's self-defense are related, yet quite different.

TRANSFORMING
THE VICTIM ROLE

Karla Grant

Women's self-defense is an issue that this culture has addressed in a myriad of ways. This essay addresses the concept of choice for women regarding their personal safety as opposed to a traditional socialization process that teaches women to be victims and then to internalize the blame for the offender's behavior. This essay also looks at the inappropriate assumption of most physical self-defense that perpetuates the myth that one has to be stronger than an assailant to neutralize him. Truth and options are a more appropriate model for self-defense instruction than a model based on mythology and denial of one's birth (civil) rights.

Most women in our society have heard the statement "Don't fight back, you will just get him angry." When this statement is taken in a literal way it means subjugate your will to an offender without question, regardless of circumstances. This statement is part of the socialization process for women in our society that denies each woman the right to make a choice regarding personal safety. The interesting paradox is that the victim is then asked if she fought back. If she says no, how is she and her experience of being assaulted processed by this society? She is told that if she didn't fight back she must have wanted it. So we train women to submit to violence, and then blame them for doing exactly what we taught them to do. Submission is synonymous with vic-

timization. It is every person's birthright to choose regarding her/his personal safety. This is the right to self-preservation.

The 1981 statistics released by The National Council on the Control and Prevention of Rape say that <u>four out of five women who fight back get out of a situation. What happens to those who submit as directed? They are</u> victimized. Our culture does not allow women a choice (i.e., fight or submit), nor does it teach them a choice that is more likely to maintain their safety (i.e., fighting back). Instead our culture tells women to submit to violence (i.e., passively accept being victimized), and then blames them for the assault and submitting to it.

This type of indoctrination perpetuates an imbalance in the rearing process that reinforces victim mentality in women and offender mentality in men. Two primary philosophical points should replace this current teaching, which is intrinsically inane and morally irresponsible. The first point is that self-preservation is a birthright to all human beings and cannot be removed by virtue of gender. Any training that teaches submission to violence does not respect the fact that every human being is the ultimate authority on her/himself since it is that person who incurs the repercussion of that decision. This means that fighting or submitting should be every individual's choice rather than assumed behaviors that the culture teaches based on gender. In our society we deny the right of self-preservation to women by teaching them they have no choice but to submit.

The second point is that we must no longer ask the victim to take responsibility for the offender's behavior by having her internalize the blame for the incident. What did she do wrong? This "blame the victim" attitude teaches women that they are responsible for men's behavior, an extremely inappropriate situation. Women are no more responsible for men's behavior than men are for women's behavior. There is no other crime in our culture where we blame the victim for the offender's behavior. Since every individual is responsible for what she/he does, victims are not responsible for an offender's behavior. The offender is responsible for his own behavior.

When our culture pauses and questions the intensity of statistics representing violence against women, we must examine the socialization process as a vehicle for generating the conditions that create such statistics. We can't continue to teach a woman to do nothing when a man attempts to violate her, and then tell the man it is the woman who is responsible for what he has done to her. Is there any question why women accept victimization and offenders expect exoneration since society supports, and in fact creates, these two mentalities? Instead our society needs to teach both genders equally that (1) every individual has the birthright to self-preservation (i.e., self-defense), and (2) every individual is responsible for his/her own behavior. This approach would allow women a choice concerning personal safety rather than making being female synonymous with victimization, and it would stop exonerating offenders from responsibility for their behavior.

Practices in this society (legal, medical, etc.) will not change until the social thought that promotes imbalances in these practices is transformed. Thought is a precursor to action or behavior. Dysfunctional thought enables and creates dysfunctional behavior. Any society that trains half its population to subjugate their will to the other half, and then exonerates the other half of behavioral accountability, is at least dysfunctional. The key to proper self-defense is to transform the traditional socialization process within each person and within the society. This transformation would make the need for psychological self-defense obsolete because the culture would begin to promote socialization that is based in morality and logic rather than prejudice of form such as gender. Self-defense must include empowerment because women's socialization process disempowers them.

An appropriate psychological unit is a critical foundation to a self-defense class. If someone (a woman) is unwilling to use physical technique it does not matter if she is able. Therefore non-victim mentality is a precursor to physical instruction. The primary incorrect assumption that permeates many physical self-defense classes is that the defender must be stronger than the offender. If a woman is being choked by a man, it is inappropriate to teach her a self-defense technique that clears his arms off her neck. For this technique to work, the woman must be stronger than the man who has her locked in a choke hold. It would be more appropriate to teach her to strike to a vital target area (eyes, groin, etc.) thereby causing the offender's grip to release due to incapacitation. This type of technique would be effective on a male offender whether or not the woman defending herself is stronger than he. All self-defense techniques should be practical and effective in a street situation. This includes not teaching women martial technique that is classically based and does not transfer to a street situation. A smaller woman can physically neutralize a larger male assailant if she has been trained properly.

It is important when selecting a self-defense class to find one that addresses these psychological and physical issues. Conveniences, such as where or when the class meets, are not as important as receiving a proper curriculum. The decision one makes regarding one's personal safety is a critical one. Do not assume that because a class is offered through a police department, college campus, martial arts school, or crisis center that the class is appropriate. Instead evaluate the curriculum based on the criterion that the class include appropriate psychological and physical units. The body cannot follow where the mind doesn't go. Therefore self-defense is more a matter of transforming one's thought rather than just learning a physical technique. This transformation will facilitate the unification of mind and body at all levels and expressions of defense, be it prevention or physical confrontation.

CULTIVATING THE SENSES
FOR OPTIMAL SELF-DEFENSE

Janet Gee

In November 1990 a friend of mine was murdered. She had been jogging on a trail in a public park—a route used by hundreds of joggers, hikers, and cyclists every day. The crime occurred on a bright, sunny day. According to police, my friend was dragged off the trail and into the bushes, where she was strangled. As of this writing, six months later, there has been no arrest in this case.

My friend was a gentle woman in her mid-30's. Her favorite pastime was jogging alone each morning along this trail. For her the activity was a form of meditation. She had never studied martial arts. That, she used to say, was too violent for her peaceful approach to life. Yet such a peaceful person was subjected to a violent—and probably horrifying—death. Chances are she was engrossed in her "runner's high" when her attacker surprised her. Chances are she was totally oblivious to the danger that lurked in her environment that day.

Since my friend was murdered, I have been rethinking my approach to teaching self-defense classes for women. I have wondered whether any of my female martial arts students would have been able to defend themselves against such a brutal attack. And I have reached the conclusion that self-defense classes for women need to include more than the routine drills that teach students how to kick and hit an assailant. I now realize that a

77

good self-defense pro-gram includes psycho-logical drills that enhance a student's awareness of her environment and give her some sensory tactics to supplement her self-defense arsenal. In the remainder of this article, I want to share some of my approach to this new way of work-ing with women in my self-defense classes.

I have targeted three special areas to focus on in the psychological part of my self-defense class-es. These three areas are the cultivation of (1) vi-sion, (2) hearing, and (3) intuition. Each area of training is designed to cultivate an expand-ed awareness of the environment and to use this awareness as a self-defense tool.

In the vision training, I teach students the value of using the eyes as a self-defense weapon. Yes, the eyes can be an effective weapon. One need only recall the old saying that someone "looked daggers at me." A piercing look can be devastating to a would-be assailant if used properly. And the ability to take in a wide area through peripheral vision can prove effective in helping a woman avoid a potentially dangerous situation. The first tech-nique involves a narrowing of focus, while the second requires an expansion of the visual field.

Here is an exercise I use with my students to help them devel-op visual self-defense: Face toward a mirror. Look directly at your eyes in the mirror. Look through the eyes in the mirror. As you do this, observe your breathing. Breathe into your center—that area below your navel—as you look through the eyes in the mirror. With your eyes penetrate the eyes that are reflected back at you in the mirror. Use the energy of the breath from your power center to look through the eyes in the mirror.

This exercise can help the student cultivate a penetrating look that comes from her power center. Being able to "stare down" a potential assailant might help eliminate the threat of becoming a victim.

After having the students use a mirror to cultivate what I call "warrior eyes," I have them pair off with partners and practice staring each other down. This is followed by feedback from the partners about possible ways of improving the warrior eyes, as well as sharing any feeling of what it is like to be on the receiving end of these visual daggers. If the eyes are the "windows of the soul," a would-be assailant might think twice before trying to assault a woman with the eyes of a warrior.

To help my students cultivate a greater awareness of the environment, I have them practice "soft eyes" exercises. Again the student breathes into her power center. But instead of allowing the eyes to focus on a particular object, she is instructed to let her eyes relax and observe those objects that enter her field of vision. When her eyes are relaxed, what are the objects she sees in the corner of her eyes? As she learns to take in a wider segment of her environment through this cultivation of peripheral vision, she can become more aware of any dangers that might lurk beside an isolated trail or a dimly lit street.

The ears can also be a valuable self-defense weapon. Simply cultivating her awareness of the sounds around her might save a woman from a would-be attacker. Again the focus is on hearing sounds in the environment by fine-tuning the sense of hearing. I have the student breathe into her power center as she simply observes the sounds in the room. The breathing keeps her centered in her power and calms the mind while her ears serve as antennae that scan the environment. I also have her "hear the directions." The student closes her eyes and breathes into her power center, then tries to identify the direction from which a sound comes. I move about the room making sounds—some soft, some loud—while she trains at identifying the sound's direction. This exercise, when practiced regularly, will help her recognize subtle shifts in sounds that might alert her to potential danger.

I also advise my students not to walk or jog alone while listening to a portable stereo. They need to be aware of the sounds in their environment, not to obliterate them with their favorite music.

It is relatively easy for the student to cultivate the visual and auditory skills described above. Cultivating the intuition is a more difficult task. Yet the ability to use one's intuition effectively is, I feel, the best self-defense skill. An intuitive person is able to "read" the potential for danger in any situation and to avert this danger without ever having to interact with it.

I use a variety of techniques to encourage my students to develop their intuition. One of the most successful techniques is to have my students simply observe their classmates and try to intuit certain characteristics about the other students.

In small groups, they observe one another and try to describe such things as the person's ways of carrying stress in the body (tightening the shoulders, clenching the jaw, etc.), the person's occupation, strengths and weaknesses, and a variety of other factors that might give some insight into who the person really is as a human being.

At first the air is usually filled with laughter and raised eyebrows as students guess wildly about characteristics and behaviors. But once the students begin to use their skills of observation, they begin to increase their accurate descriptions of characteristics. Developing intuition involves developing the ability to observe to its highest degree. And a highly tuned intuition—the proverbial sixth sense—allows a person to be a warrior of the highest degree.

Of course, in my self-defense classes for women I do not neglect those valuable skills of punching and kicking and shouting and using everyday objects as weapons against a would-be attacker. These ingredients are basic to any self-defense program. But I find that by having my students cultivate their visual and auditory senses and develop their intuition, their punches and kicks become more devastating, their screams become more piercing and fierce, and their use of ordinary objects as self-defense weapons becomes more powerful. In short, I feel that this combination of the psychological with the physical better prepares my students for any assault.

I still grieve for my friend who was murdered as she pursued her form of meditation. But I have some peace of mind knowing that her death has made me even more determined to help women become warriors rather than victims.

ONE STAGE OF THE ROAD: AN INTERVIEW WITH LIDIA ALEXANDRA WOLANSKYJ

Conducted by Sharon McGowan, filmmaker

Sharon McGowan approached Lidia as an instructor of Aikido to participate in a film on women in the martial arts, but the film was later limited to 20 minutes and the focus had to be restricted to karate, Sharon's form of martial arts training. They taped an interview, which Lidia later transcribed and edited, but which was never published. The following is a condensed version of that interview.

S: Can you tell me about Aikido? How is it good for self-defense and, well, what is it?

L: Aikido is definitely long-term ongoing practice, because its whole function, according to its founder, is to help people fundamentally change the way they deal with the world.

Morihei Ueshiba, like the founders of many modern martial arts, was a Japanese man. He died in 1969, in his late eighties. What I've always found interesting is the kind of things he would say about martial arts, which they refer to as *Budo* in Japanese. He had studied along the same lines as any man, going through very 'macho' phases, going through this thing about having to prove himself for these and those and other reasons. Then, during the Second World War he went into retreat—at that point he was in his late fifties—and came out after the war and began to call his art Aiki-Do, instead of Aiki-Jitsu, which is what it used to be.

And what he said was: "True Budo knows of no opponent or an enemy. True Budo seeks to join itself with the center of the universe, which is divine love."

Of course some of his senior students thought "Oh, the old man has gone soft, I'm going to break off and do my own so-and-so style Aikido from now on. I don't want to have anything to do with this mushy stuff!" That was where all the splits began to happen, which is not unusual.

But what was amazing was that he, as a Japanese, possibly partly because of Japan's defeat in the Second World War, had a real awareness and illumination about the whole issue of fighting: that if you are constantly seeking to overcome your enemies, you are doomed to defeat, because there will always be somebody stronger than you, somewhere in the world. As a nation Japan experienced that very severely, and as an individual he realized that and decided to do something different with his art.

So the focus in Aikido is always to try and work through things within yourself. To use forms and kata and technique to move your body always in relation to what's going on around you. So you can't just perfect it as a solo trip, and feel "Okay, I've accomplished everything there is to accomplish." There's always that other energy you have to deal with, that other reality beyond yourself, that's impinging on you. The way you react to it is such an image of who you are, and how you deal with the world, and how you see yourself.

One of metaphors I like for training in Aikido is that your partner is a mirror, and you use your partner to polish yourself. So it's a constant process of trying to improve on what it is that you yourself are doing, through the process of working with another person.

People's reactions to an attack tell you so much about where they're coming from. Take me, starting out at the age of 22 as your classic, unathletic bookworm: I saw myself on video about a month and a half after I started doing Aikido, and it was the most embarrassing and revealing thing that I had ever seen of myself.

There I was, running scared around the mat. I was supposed to be doing a strike to the head, just a plain open-handed blow to the

middle of the forehead, and I kept backing off. I was cowering behind my arm! Rather than putting out energy and giving the other person something to work with, I was cowering as if I was the one being hit! As I watched, I realized that I just couldn't cope with the idea of trying to hit another person. I couldn't even look like I was trying to hit them. It was such a shock to me, to see this wimpy, mousey person backing away from people instead of giving them energy that they could learn from. I had no choice but start to change: I ended up crying for about an hour at that workshop and spent a lot of time talking to one of the younger teachers, just trying to come to terms with what I had seen.

I think that for many people, it is very scary that in Aikido they may have to start dealing with emotional stuff. I'm sure it comes up in other arts, but I only know about Aikido. I've seen both women and men quit because they didn't want to have to deal with that. The physical stuff was okay; they could handle that. But they didn't want to have to deal with how they were looking at the world, or how they were relating to other people. That was too frightening.

But it's inevitable: if you're doing something intense like Aikido, on a long-term basis, it's not just dealing with physical realities, it's dealing with how you are in this world.

There is often quite a difference between the women and men who come in who haven't done a lot of other physical activities. The women tend to be very loose, very relaxed. There's no resistance, not even much presence very often. So they don't usually get hurt because when something happens they just flop down on the floor, and that's okay, at the beginning. The men, on the other hand, very often come with a certain amount of "Well, this is self-defense, I guess I'm supposed to be strong and hard and make it tough for people." So people are often tougher on them, and they're more likely to get hurt at the beginning.

Then, what starts happening is this: the women may go through a few months of being limp and loose, and after a while the practice isn't very satisfying: not much is there, not much is happening. They are almost a non-presence in the movement. When they are the attacker, they can 'get away with it,' to some extent, because then the other person will just manipulate them and throw them around and do something to them. But when they're the defender and they're that limp, they just find themselves being blocked over and over again. In other words, if the other person's energy has any power in it and the defender isn't present, she just gets—

S: —run over?

L: —stopped. Over and over again. The defender gets stopped, and she sometimes literally gets 'run over.' It's really fascinating to me as a teacher, because I go around the class and I work out with people, and I can see, almost overnight sometimes, in a woman, that suddenly there's something there! And it's amazing how powerful—when these unathletic women choose to let the power come out—how powerful they can be.

85

In general, with the men it's a different thing. They're used to using their muscles. So it's much harder to see them get over their initial hump, which is to stop depending on all the biceps and triceps and pecs to get things happening for them. There's constant blocking, aggressing—you know—imposition of will. That's usually a lot harder, in a way, to deal with, because I think most of the women can come up with power fairly early in their training. But for the men to let go of force as a way of dealing with life is a lot harder. It's a longer process for many of them. Because they are strong, I guess for many of them it's still very rewarding to be doing Aikido, so they generally hang in there.

You know, everything that you do on the mats translates so immediately into what's going on in your regular life.

S: Can you give me some examples?

L: Say somebody comes to grab your hand. You collapse and pull into yourself, but at the same time there's a hardness there—like you're not yielding, but you're collapsing because you want to get the attacker close and control the situation—you usually end up being blocked. What you've done is allowed that person so much into your space, and you've pulled them so close that you no longer have enough space to do anything.

For instance, you're in a situation where somebody wants to be confrontive with you. If you decide to respond with aggression yourself, to try to control that person with your own confrontiveness, and you haven't maintained sufficient distance, you get so caught up in it, that more often than not, you are defeated. Because people who come on strong in a negative way, who are confrontive and aggressive in public situations, are usually very good at it. That's why they do it! If you don't know what you're doing and you decide to be heavy back, you usually get completely screwed up. They win because they know what they're doing. People like that are very powerful in this stance; being heavy with other people is their way of feeling good in the world, and they're very good at it.

So the only way to deal with confrontive, aggressive people in Aikido terms is to keep your distance, maintain your personal space. You don't try to absorb into you something that you can't deal with. In Aikido movements, it translates as *tae-no-tenkan*: usually if the attack is very strong, you turn. You turn away from the onslaught to give yourself space and time to deal with it. It's generally harder and requires much better timing, much more presence to do direct, entering movements, or *irimi*. It's much easier to turn and oblige the attacker to come around again while you set yourself up for a response.

It's exactly the same thing in life. If someone's really aggressive and strong, there's no point in attempting to deal with them directly, in giving back exactly what they're giving you, because they're going to win.

S: So do you think your martial art is the answer to world peace?

L: No. I think each art suits different people.

S: In what way?

L: I think physically, mentally, and emotionally the arts appeal to different people and satisfy different things for people. I don't think it's possible for any one system to be the answer to anything.

S: Diversity is a good thing?

L: Oh yes, people are so different. If we were all similar, we wouldn't have the kind of world that we have. Everybody would, in fact, be doing one thing; it's a truism. Luckily, people are drawn to different things. Some people look at Aikido and they growl: "Bah, that's really wimpy!" or they cringe: "Oh god, look at those flips!" Other people look at Aikido and fall in love with it. It all depends on what somebody is prepared to deal with.

A lot of people come and go. Aikido has a lot less glamour value, because it is less-known, it's not competitive, you don't win trophies in it, you can't go in a bar and punch somebody's lights out with your Aikido training. I mean, some people might do that, but it wouldn't be Aikido, and I don't think those people would be wasting their time doing Aikido, they'd probably be doing something else.

The process of learning to deal with aggression is painful and long. I still haven't been able to apply Aikido principles in my own life nearly the way that I'd like to. I still find myself reacting defensively to people, particularly in verbal situations. I don't just mean when someone aggressively confronts me—that's a situation where many people feel a little threatened—but for instance, when a group of people are bantering at a party: I want to be able to keep up with it, I want to sound just as witty and clever as the next person. There's a certain amount of aggressiveness in that.

S: There's a lot of aggressiveness in that!

L: Sure, depending on the group of people and how much ego is involved, that can become extremely aggressive and even ugly. But I'm talking about even relatively benign situations. I find myself wanting to be 'just as good as' the next person, and my ego will get caught up in it, and there are times when I know I just have to pull myself up by the collar and say, "Hey, lay back and listen for a while. Don't feel like you have to answer everything that happens around you."

That whole business of not responding to every single overture that the universe makes toward you—that's an issue that came up for my senior student recently when he was trying to do freestyle. In Aikido we don't have competitive activities; we don't have people sparring with each other; but what we do have, as you get more advanced, is a single person being attacked or set upon by more than one person. It's generally called randori or multiple-attack freestyle.

Most people, when they first start doing that, feel: "Oh god, I've got to do an Aikido technique on every person that touches me!" That's ridiculous! Many of the standard techniques are fairly complicated and require space, require self-possession, just require a great deal of skill. When you have three or four people jumping you, you don't have the time or the space to do perfectly executed classic *waza*. It takes people a long time to figure out, "Wait a minute! If this person's just being a milquetoast, kind of grabbing onto my shirt and hanging on very loosely, why do I have to do something to them? They're obviously not very serious about attacking... I can just stick my hand in their face and move on to the next person." Or, "Maybe I can just get out of the line of attack, this time." It's very applicable to real life.

There's no reason to respond at the same level to every little thing that impinges on you. There are a lot of things that you can just brush off like a fly landing on your shoulder. In a way, that's the kind of attitude that you want to develop. I think that if more people had that kind of attitude, there would be a real difference in whether the world had peace or not. You know, if every person who got hassled in a bar were able to just kind of brush it off pleasantly and move on, and do their own thing, we'd have far fewer bar brawls, for sure. It's taming the attitude that "Oh god, somebody challenged me, threatened me, scared me, I've got to smash them to smithereens."

S: So for the advanced student, it wasn't so much a technique issue, because he'd already reached a certain level, it was just a fine tune.

L: You're right, it wasn't technique, it was the way that he was responding to the situation. One teacher of Aikido put it in a way that I found very effective: "When somebody attacks you, turn and face the world, and look at it the way that they're seeing it." In the process of doing that, of course, you get out of the way of the attack . . .

One of the reasons Aikido has never been competitive is that it could be quite deadly if it were. If people were doing it to 'get at' each other, it would present a whole different attitude. Most of the time in your Aikido training, what you're doing is creating openings, finding and using vulnerable points in your partner's attack. Your partner, in turn, should look for vulnerable points in your posture and movement.

I have a feeling that most of the martial arts have that same philosophy: that it's better to evade and control, than it is to answer force with force. But on the surface, when you're dealing with competition, you don't get points for avoiding in Judo, you don't get points for keeping your distance in karate or Tae Kwon Do; you get points for throwing somebody, you get points for hitting them.

Those arts have a lot to offer, and they have different things to offer from what Aikido offers; and yet for somebody who doesn't want to increase the amount of competitiveness in themselves and in their lives and in the people around them, I imagine that it would be very hard to reconcile that concept of "having to do something to somebody else" in order to be considered successful.

So much of aggressiveness is posturing. I think you can learn so much about the way the world is functioning from these things. Martial arts are all a microcosm of what's going on out there. Even a thing like the warm-ups can be very revealing. One of the women in my dojo discovered that her knee was hyperflexible. It overextended, and every once in a while the joint simply popped out, and then she couldn't straighten out her leg for a few minutes. What it came down to was that her body was overly flexible. And that over-flexibility caused her problems: it made her weak; it made her joints unstable.

To me this is an incredible metaphor for over-flexibility in a female personality: when women are so willing to adapt, to effectively give in, all the time, that they have no stability, have no power, and just get run over, either by their own instability or by the aggression of others.

The parallels are just amazing, and it's so valuable to be working on these issues at a physical level, because it's really difficult to start significant change simply on a psychological level. In fact, it's almost impossible to 'talk' yourself into any kind of real change. But if you start dealing with physical activities that you're involved in, with what your body feels like, it's almost always a reflection of the rest your life. So this woman is working now on that knee, on developing strength and a certain amount of rigidity and resistance. Because without that resistance, that strength, her knee is going to pop out constantly: she'll never be able to feel confident in it, she'll never have strength or stability in it, and in the end she might even need surgery.

Think about it: we always admire babies for being so flexible—they can put their toes in their ears and this kind of stuff—it's great, but the baby's not trying to do with its body what we're trying to do with ours. That baby can't walk, when it's that flexible—

S: It can't lead a life of its own!

L: It can't walk, it can't run, it's not independent in any way, shape or form. It's merely very flexible and jelly-like. And that's that.

S: And it's liked by everyone. (laughter)

L: It has to learn resistance; it has to learn to control its muscles and to pay the price of having less flexibility, for more stability, more mobility, and more independence. You can't have it all.

S: I have the opposite problem. I have too much rigidity, and yet I don't like to fight. It's amazing how people's personalities really come out in a martial art. I wouldn't do well in a very aggressive *dojo* precisely because I think I'm too aggressive, and I don't like to have to deal with it.

L: I think that often happens, that people who are very conscious about aggression and feel they have a lot of it, go to the other extreme and really try to suppress it. So it may be better for such a person to be somewhere where people don't make a big deal out of aggression and a person can let it out and feel safe. That's what I like about Aikido. I'm somewhat aggressive myself, in the sense of wanting things my own way, being assertive and so on. I'm not necessarily always comfortable with being assertive, but just determined when something really matters, having the attitude "Well, I want it this way, and I know I might trample on so-and-so's toes, and some people aren't going to like me much, but I want to have it this way."

So for me, doing Aikido is a way of playing out that aggression. I don't have to worry that if I throw my partner, I win and they lose, or if they throw me, I lose, because it's mutual. It's always back and forth. We're playing roles, and it's acknowledged that it's roles. That's the difference in a competitive art. In competition it's no longer a question of playing roles. You're both out to win; and one of you is going to win, and one of you is going to lose, because that's the way it's been set up.

But when you're playing a role, you take away that element of competitiveness, of win and loss, it becomes enjoyable. I can throw you twenty times, you can throw me twenty-five, I don't care. We're both learning, and nobody's counting. I can get all my aggression out and nobody gives a hoot because we're having fun doing it.

To me, the ideal is to have a situation where everybody can do the best possible, but nobody 'wins' at the expense of anyone else. A situation where you all basically can walk away feeling "Wow, I was terrific! I really did my best and it was great!" Nobody's walking away feeling, "Oh, so-and-so did better than me and I'm lousy, blah blah blah." That's something that will take a lifetime for most of us to get out of our systems, to accept who we are, and work with that.

S: How about self-defense? How do you feel about things like women's self defense, in relation to what you're doing?

L: Well again, I think there is some particular area that every form of martial art addresses itself to, that is less obvious in all the others, and that's why it is developed and that's why people study it. I think special women's self-defense training can be really good for helping women who have been traumatized; to allow some of their anger out very aggressively and very directly— because they do full-contact punching and kicking into bags and a lot of *ki-ai*; it's a very safe environment because the students are working out only with other women, and they don't have to be confronted with their unresolved feelings about men and their feelings of victimization in front of men. This kind of training can be very effective in situations of sudden danger: it teaches very specific jiu-jutsu-like techniques that you can use against someone immediately: stepping on the metatarsal arch, kicking a man in the balls, jabbing someone in the throat, eye or nostrils, whatever. These are really basic, aggressive things that a woman can learn to do if she feels seriously threatened in the streets: women who work at night, women who have been molested, women who live in areas that aren't particularly safe and have to constantly be traversing them alone.

Aikido is not going to offer those kinds of immediate results. That is, people feel benefits almost immediately, but they're much subtler. They're much more psychological, but they're working through the body. The surface effect may be simply, for many women, to feel a lot more aware of how strong they can be. To me, that's more effective as long-term, real self-defense, which is not needing self-defense. My teacher, Saotome Sensei, often quotes Teddy Roosevelt: "Speak softly and carry a big stick." To me, this means having established such a strong sense of who you are within yourself, establishing your personal space, having this—to use an Aikido metaphor—sphere of energy around you, that people can sense it. People who want to hurt you, people who are about to bump into you, will sense: "There's presence here. This is not territory that's open to invasion; I'd better move around it. It's something I have to reckon with. It's something that's there and present; I can't ignore it." At that point you're not even talking about learning to be aggressive, you're talking about *being there*. Being really present within yourself, not being 'out to lunch' with a little sign, so that people can just walk in and walk off with stuff, be it your space or your sexuality, your emotions, your money, your life . . . whatever.

That's why I think that a long-term training is probably more fundamentally beneficial training for most people. If you're feeling immediate pressure, immediate feelings of anger or threat that have to be dealt with, I think it's good to do a course that offers short-term, immediate results, like Wendo[1] or Model Mugging.[2] But it's also really good either to continue with more advanced courses in that self-defense, or to get into some more traditional form of martial art that will give you an ongoing support for growing in personal strength.

It's not enough to learn that you can hurt someone twenty-three different ways in five seconds flat if they jump you. If you don't feel good about yourself, if you're not confident within yourself, if you haven't got a sense of having a right to the territory that you occupy, then no amount of technique, no bag of little tricks is going to help, because you aren't going to react properly when push comes to shove. When someone aggresses on you, you're going to immediately assume again that they have a

---

[1]Wendo is a type of self-defense designed specifically for women and the types of attacks they are likely to encounter.

[2]Model Mugging is a women's self-defense and empowerment program that offers full-contact training.

right to your territory, that they can invade your space and take over, because you don't deserve it.

It takes so long for most of us just to be able to make a punch and go *whoomm*, and have a sense that we've actually punched, as opposed to floating our fist through the air to a certain point somewhere in front of us.

S: That's right, and not feeling that we have to apologize for it, but rather that we take responsibility for the action.

Speaking of responsibility, I heard a self-defense success story about a woman who had taken Wendo. She was attacked in the classic street way, walking home late at night. And she took out the attacker's eye. But as I listened to the story, I thought: A few years ago, I would have agreed that this was a success story, but now I'm not so sure. In one way, I still feel that it is, in that there was no violence perpetrated on this woman, that the man was stopped and will probably think twice before he goes after another woman. In that sense it's a success story. But at the same time, I don't know how I would feel if I took out somebody's eye. I think that I might wish I'd had the choice to stop him—

L: —without doing that.

S: —without having to do that, which, as you say, takes a lot of skill and a lot of training. Not everyone can get to that point. It's a real achievement.

L: It is. I remember years ago reading that, in terms of Budo, the martial arts, there are four ethical levels of development. The lowest level is people who have an aggressive attitude toward the world and run around killing and maiming others, be it physically or otherwise. The second level is people who incite others to attack them so that they can turn around and be justified in beating, maiming or even murdering their attacker. This is your standard barroom brawl mentality. The third level is people who don't go around encouraging any violence or egging anybody on to attack them, but if somebody does, they will immediately pulverize them. The highest level is the level of people who not only do not encourage any kind of aggressive behavior around them but who, when it does happen, redirect it and cause as little harm as possible. Ideally, that's the aim of Aikido.

Yet, if your only impression of Aikido is a Steven Segal film, Aikido's ethics don't seem any higher than 3, at best, on the scale.

A lot of martial arts schools seem to encourage people to be very competitive and aggressive, although traditionally there was a strong ethical attitude in every art. Like you, I think that gouging somebody's eye out, unless they are about to kill me, is not my idea of a success story, ultimately. Yet for now, I would rather hear of that, than hear of women who are not succeeding in doing it, and are being raped and mutilated.

We're on the way; this is one stage of the road.

TRANSFERENCE, COUNTERTRANSFERENCE, AND THE GURU-SENSEI: A FEMINIST THERAPIST'S VIEW OF THE SENSEI-STUDENT RELATIONSHIP

Marilyn May

Who would have expected to find it in the women's martial arts community? But there it is: sensei worship. Some martial arts students will do anything for their sensei, inside or outside the *dojo*, on or off the mats.

Of course this is not so in all schools, but it is not uncommon to meet students who are fiercely loyal to their instructors—who defend or protect them, make sizeable personal or material donations to them, or go to extremes to win their approval. Some students go so far as to imitate the values, lifestyles, and even hairstyles of their instructors.

In truth, to learn a martial art one must have a certain amount of trust in and dedication to one's teacher—a willingness to abandon old ways and be shown new ways. Serious training requires some loyalty to one's art, one's *dojo,* and one's instructor. But there is a danger in giving too much reverence, and a price to pay for this mistake.

Many senseis are highly principled people who strive to live rightly. Others are not. In either case, it is a big responsibility to be adored by one's students and to be emulated in areas beyond the realm of martial arts. Some teachers are unable to accept such adulation, keep it in perspective, and resist letting it get to their heads. Once perspective is lost, the relationship becomes tainted, and the student inevitably suffers.

In Asian cultures, from which most martial arts came, the social structure keeps the sensei-student relationship appropriate. Cultural norms govern a permanently unequal relationship. There are models of such relationships in how younger generations treat their elders and in how certain groups in society behave with other groups. But in American culture, where students and instructors are often of the same generation and the same community, false lines of demarcation may be drawn, while appropriate ones may be ignored. While a permanently unequal relationship can be maintained in the *dojo,* no cultural foundation exists for this relationship outside the *dojo.* And it is outside the *dojo* where many sensei-student relationships go wrong.

In our society, there are many examples of healthy teacher-student relationships. The roles in these relationships are well defined, the duration is usually limited, and the purposes of the relationships are specific. For school children and their teachers, the natural line of demarcation is that the student is much younger than the teacher. In colleges, universities, training programs, and adult schools the relationship between student and professor is temporary and the purpose is clear. The student has paid a fee to be taught a certain skill or subject; nothing more.

In the *dojo,* however, the duration of the training is not specified and it is usually expected to be very long-term. The subject matter is more than just physical, it is sometimes philosophical and often spiritual. Obedience, loyalty, and even subservience to the instructor are encouraged or required. The physical and spiritual aspects of the martial arts add a unique intensity to the relationship between the teacher and the student.

This kind of relationship is almost unparalleled in our society. Two exceptions come to mind. The first is the clergy-parishioner relationship in religious communities. This relationship is long-term, it is permanently unequal, and it is spiritual, powerful, and intense. This relationship is governed by centuries of well-developed, well-defined rules and cultural norms, taught by each generation to the next. Occasions in history when this rela-

tionship has been abused offer proof of the intensity of the relationship and the importance of the norms that govern it.

The second exception is the therapist-client relationship. The psychotherapeutic relationship is usually open-ended or long-term, it is unequal, it is instantly intimate and therefore very intense, and it is purposely vague or unspecific about the scope of the subjects it will address. Although it is relatively new in its current form, it is governed by a large body of literature and a strict code of ethics. Therapists must be trained, licensed, and monitored by their peers. Established procedures address abuses that occur.

Psychotherapists recognize and acknowledge the importance and power of the relationship between therapist and client. Therapists are trained to understand the transference issues of the client—the characteristics the client projects onto the therapist, often borrowed from the client's previous experiences. Therapists also must acknowledge countertransference issues—the feelings evoked *in* the therapist *about* the client, usually in response to the projected characteristics. Attention to these issues is fundamental to therapy. Transference is a tool the therapist must study and understand in order to use it to teach clients about themselves. To take the transference relationship beyond the boundaries of the sessions would render it useless as a therapeutic tool and turn the tool to destructive use. Therapists are trained to treat the relationship responsibly, not allowing it to go beyond its prescribed

boundaries. An understanding of countertransference lets therapists recognize false feelings of self-importance that occur in
response to the transference. This understanding helps them resist
any temptation to violate the boundaries of the therapeutic relationship.

The sensei-student relationship is no less powerful and no less
subject to abuse. It deserves no less understanding and attention.
Of course, the goals of therapy and martial arts training are entirely different. Instructors are not expected to address or remedy
the failures in a student's childhood. But there are parallels
between the two kinds of relationship. Students frequently put
their senseis on pedestals and imbue them with larger-then-life
personal characteristics, as clients do their therapists. A certain
mystery surrounds the sensei, and the therapist, as if each holds
knowledge and power unattainable by others. In therapy, this
leads to healthy exploration of transference feelings. In martial
arts training, it leads to falsely exaggerated inequality between
student and teacher that may extend beyond training.

When this perceived inequality is carried outside the *dojo*,
training suffers and people can be hurt. *Dojo* rules may be bent,
and the distinction between training time and social time may
be lost. The line between sensei as sensei, and sensei as friend,
neighbor, or even lover may be blurred. More seriously, students'
feelings of self-worth may diminish, as they give up their power
and self-approval to their teacher. Meanwhile, the sensei's own
feeling of self-worth may be artificially inflated, as she accepts
the power projected onto her that rightfully belongs to the student. Worse still, when the sensei is not a principled person qual-
ified for the job of guru, students who set out to learn martial
arts may end up giving their loyalty and dedication to dishon-
orable causes.

What is the solution? Should black belt requirements include
psychotherapy training? If true love or true friendship happen
to come along during martial arts training, must the parties
involved abandon their martial arts careers? Of course not. The
solution is simple. Every martial arts instructor must be aware
of the pedestal phenomenon. She or he must resist the tempta-

tion to take adoration personally and make an effort to demystify the role of sensei. When instructors choose to socialize with students outside of class, they must do so on equal footing, not expecting loyalty or deference beyond that of equal friendship. They also must be able to be instructors again, once inside the *dojo*. Rank—and power—of one person over another should exist only within the four walls of the *dojo*.

Let us remember, for a moment, good old-fashioned feminism. As women martial artists we must ask ourselves: When a relationship diminishes our self-worth in order to support another person's power, is this a healthy relationship for us? Are we so starved for strong role models that we make cult heros of our instructors, instead of simply learning the martial arts they know?

One school of psychotherapy has a concept that is useful when we look at the unique relationship between instructors and martial arts students. Feminist therapists recognize that some relationships are necessarily unequal. Parent and child, teacher and student, therapist and client—these are unequal relationships. But feminist therapists believe that *healthy* unequal relationships are *temporarily* unequal. The therapist restores a client to health and to equality with the therapist. The parent raises the child to become his equal in adulthood. The teacher or sensei shares her knowledge with the student in order for the student to master the art, just as the sensei did.

For women martial artists, both students and instructors, there are lessons to be learned from the principles of feminist therapy. Temporary inequality can be the basis for a healthy, non-degrading relationship for the sensei and the student. While expertise and rank should be respected, they ought not be exalted. A respectful, temporarily unequal relationship leaves no room for worship and disappointment. There is no reason to perpetuate unequal relationships that serve egotistical purposes outside the scope of martial arts.

Instructors should acknowledge the importance of, and potential risks in, their relationships with their students. Instructors should respect the boundaries of their roles in the relationship and be able to recognize and handle the pedestal phenomenon. As therapists do, martial arts instructors must recognize false feelings of self-importance for what they are, and resist the temptation to blur the boundaries of their roles inside and outside the *dojo.*

Students also must bear some responsibility. As an adult and as a woman, a student must not give up her power easily. She should choose a teacher who practices principles similar to her own, or she should choose to learn from her teacher only the martial arts that the teacher has mastered.

The *dojo* is a place where one can learn more than physical techniques. Let these lessons be learned in an environment of dignity and mutual respect. Those who are grounded strongly enough in their own strength are able to maintain their dignity, self-respect, and appropriate personal power, as students or as senseis.

WOMEN
TRAINING WOMEN

Anne Moon

It is worth turning a critical eye on the process of students in the martial arts becoming teachers of martial artists. For all teachers, especially for women teachers, it is important to examine the relationships we have with both our students and our teachers. Enough women have trained and have taught their own students that we must look carefully at how we have tried to change the teacher/student relationship and at the kinds of teaching models we have used to make these changes.

I have trained for eighteen years and taught for twelve. I am a second generation black belt in all-women schools. My main teachers trained under men in primarily male-dominated schools then started and ran primarily all-female schools. I have watched my own and other instructors' students become black belts and begin their own classes, promote their own students, and make their own ethical and aesthetic choices in Martial Arts. And so it continues: "Women training women," as Pye Bateman[1] has said, "for a better world."

[1]Pye Bateman is founder of Feminist Karate Union and Alternatives to Fear Self Defense Organization, both in Seattle, WA. She is one of the first to pioneer all-womens' classes and she continues to tie in the political and social implications of violence, abuse, and harassment in the workplace.

During this process of training, we have wanted to be more "feminist" and/or less patriarchal, without sacrificing the historical or spiritual significance of the martial arts. In the most traditional model of teaching, the master addressed the senior student and this student led the class. Access to the master was limited and earned by years of hard training. Military decorum and "martial" bearing often typified the school's atmosphere. Changing and adapting this model to women's schools has been no easy task. But if we look at the number of women attending all-women conferences who are black belts teaching in their own schools, it seems obvious that many of us are trying to do something different from the traditional model.

We can grow as teachers, student teachers, and students training together. We can also grow by examining our process together. Many schools have adopted group process and criticism from the Civil Rights and Feminist movements of the 60's and 70's. Recovery work, so prominent among us in the 80's and 90's, is also influencing our training and school process. Recovery work has encouraged us to examine the influences of addictive and dysfunctional behavior, past and present, on our present learning behavior and teaching relationships. Recovery work also reminds us that we are teaching adults, who come to us with unique and influential experiences that require recognition and integration into their ongoing training. Keeping in mind these historical influences, let us turn a critical and honest eye on the changing and evolving teacher/student relationship.

I want to look at three models for this relationship: the family model, the sports/military model, and the creative model. In the family model, the beginner is like the baby, and the teacher is the all-nourishing, protective, and critical parent. The teacher guides, directs, protects, encourages, cajoles, pushes, or discourages the student as she grows in the art. Mom, the Head Instructor, knows best. The student grows up in the art and eventually stands on her own feet. Similar to adolescent rebellion, the student often challenges the parent teacher, tests her limits, or leaves in open disagreement to try her style elsewhere. In the history of the martial arts, students initially molded by parental-like teachers often

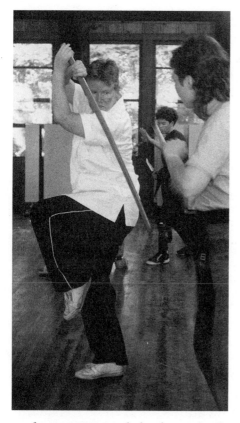

have eventually disagreed with the teacher and left to start a new style.

Certainly the commitment a teacher makes to her students can feel like a parent's commitment to raising children. The struggles and trials for both student and teacher can resemble family squabbles, dysfunctional and otherwise. However, in many ways the family model fails us as teachers. Teachers are not true parents: many of our students are as adult and mature as we are. The student wants an art form in which the teacher simply has more experience. Many of us, teachers and students, are survivors of incest, abuse, and rape or are adults from dysfunctional families. We require a learning model different from the parent/child one.

Many of us women teachers can readily articulate the fallacious aspects of the hierarchical/patriarchal approach to teaching. We know that power centralized at the top can lead to rigidity. Knowledge handed down from above can lead to passive, rote learning and can stifle individual interpretation and creativity. Older does not always mean wiser. But many teachers have nonetheless become benevolent (or not so benevolent) "mothers" to their schools, thinking this constitutes a "feminist" change, when it does not. Granted there are differences between running a school as a general would run an army or running it as a parent runs a large household. But the overall process can be similar: directorial and hierarchical, whether matriarchal or patriarchal.

A second model is the sports/combat model. This model is

prevalent when teaching the win/lose, better-than/not-so-good-as method of martial arts. In this model the teacher is a coach of many teams (ranks) who often learn by direct or indirect competition among themselves, with attendant champions or stars. The best or the hardest working or most skilled players often become coaches themselves. The kind of physical drill inherent to martial arts allows the arts to draw from and fit into the novice-to-master training of sports, games, and by extension, warfare. We are, after all, *martial* artists. Perhaps we train consciously seeking spiritual development and/or artistic perfection; but we are also striking, trapping, sweeping, throwing, controlling, and "miming" the practice of injuring and killing.

The sports model has engendered the widespread practice of tournaments and allowed martial arts to enter the Olympics. But the model has its limits as well. Martial arts are expansive and not limited by the same parameters and rules as games and sports. Teaching has some aspects of coaching but teaching martial arts requires a larger ethic than winning or losing. When the tournaments are over, and the winners and losers determined, we are still martial artists. The focus acquired during intensive kata practice may win us recognition in competition but it also will permeate and change the daily aspects of our lives as well. How do we account for this? How do we teach to accomplish this?

A third model worth considering is the creative model, in which the creation of a work of art and the relationship between the teacher and the student(s) happen simultaneously. This does not mean the teacher is a master sculptor and the student a lump of clay. Rather the martial art is like a venerable, respected ballet rechoreographed by a modern day director, with the practitioners becoming more skilled with the practice and reworking of the art. This assures the dance's (or art's) continued historical significance and continuity as well as the performers' own discipline.

Wait a minute, you say, teaching beginners to punch and kick is nothing like choreographing a dance; and you are right, it isn't. But if we teachers approach beginners and all our students with the awareness that all of us are engaged in a creative process, then the relationship of teacher to student and both to the art can evolve comfortably through stages similar to painting a picture or creating any art form. This process can ensure that women continue training themselves and others, can create good (beautiful, in fact) art, and can allow the martial arts to grow and change their schools.

In the first stages of this creative process, the painter regards the canvas; that is the student checks out the art, and the teacher considers the new student. Will this student stay? Will she try? Will the teacher like the student, will the student like the teacher or the practice of the art? The student is asking her own questions. Can I learn from this teacher, can I trust her, can I face my fear, how much of a commitment do I want to or can I realistically make?

The overall development of novice into skilled practitioner is clearer to the teacher because she has already been through this process, and as a teacher, has seen other beginners come and go. However, each beginner is certainly no baby to movement, dance, or sports, and increasingly no novice to martial arts. Each teacher and each student have their own canvases of prior successes or failures with other kinds of movement skills and competitive games, as well as other teaching relationships. Each also has her own unique learning style and social/cultural responses to the sometimes very new challenges of martial arts. If the teacher can support and maintain a creative learning environment through consistency of class material, then the ongoing structure and discipline of the Art itself can help the student get through just making it to class. She can grow to some sort of awareness of herself as an individual studying an art.

At this stage it is important for the teacher not to be confused. We teachers cajole, exhort, praise, and practice immense patience and love, but we are neither mothers, nor lovers, nor drill sergeants. A teacher's skill and expertise is seen by the beginner as a manifestation of the martial art itself. It can be very ego-gratifying for the teacher to be adored and admired from this place. But if the student is to become advanced in her training and eventually a successful teacher, she must separate the art from the teacher, embody the art within her body, refine her unique contributions to the art, and re-express the art from this new place, not just copy the teacher. Emulation is only one step on the way to becoming an individual martial artist.

For the student, the middle stage of the creative model begins with a scary inkling of herself as separate from other students and from the teacher and the art form. The art is taking a life of its own within the student. Often this occurs when other beginners come in behind her. She sees how much she has learned and also how little she knows. For the teacher, this stage is marked by a decrease in open acceptance/admiration and an increase in challenges to her leadership. The student may be craving the earlier all-embracing consistency and structure of the art form. The teacher wishes the student could just relax and train, knowing that training itself will ensure gradual development of skills and eventual mastery. But until the student is confident she is able to embody the art form in her own struggling body, it will feel like a long period of protracted struggle for both teacher and student. The student often doesn't understand why she isn't promoted. The teacher is baffled by the student's apparent inability to hear corrections or make changes. This period of training is like that point in the creation of a work of art when the form is unfinished and the artist feels lost.

But this difficult period can also be very exciting for both teacher and student. The student's own unique abilities are emerging. She knows enough basics to become creative. She sees others worth modelling besides the teacher. She sees others struggling behind her and develops an awareness of how she got to where she is. She may feel a tremendous surge of power and new gratification with her skills.

For the teacher, it can be a time of individuation as well. As she becomes less the art form itself and more the guide and supporter of each individual student's relationship to the art, she is freer to develop her own relationship to the art. The martial art and the school grow because each student brings her unique skills to both. Of lesser importance are the differences of opinion and inconsistencies between the teacher and student. The teacher models the ongoingness of the art by her individual practice. Through tests, evaluations, and rank, she maintains the standards of the art. The student works to bring her practice to a place consistent with both those standards and her own emerging personal values.

When an artist has completed her work, she steps back to regard it, and the work stands alone. This stage is reached in training when the student embraces, practices, and models the standards consistently enough to be deemed "advanced," and when she is a senior student or new teacher by virtue of her seniority to the rest of the students. If the student is already teaching beginners, then the teacher is working with both an advanced student and a new teacher. To this kind of student, the teacher is less a director and more of a colleague with greater experience, advising rather than ordering.

New issues arise at this point in the teacher/student relationship. The teacher continues to train the advanced student to achieve black belt or equivalent mastery and also helps the student realize her own goals within the art. The actual accomplishment of both these goals—once so far in the future and now so close at hand—means that both teacher and student must rethink their relationship to one another and to the school. Anxieties for the student prior to black belt are often expressed in belabored concerns for exact detail and superficial minutia of the art. The student may feel confined by the teacher's expectations and standards. Often her frustration or confusion is passed on to or acted out by the newer students in the school.

If the teacher has trouble allowing the student to stand on her own as a black belt or teacher, then she may keep changing or raising the standards, becoming mired in details or perfectionism. Both teacher and student need to relinquish their former roles. For many years of training, the teacher truly is "more experienced," but at the point of separation from her student, she becomes "differently experienced." She must stand back and let her artwork (embodied in the art of her student) pass or fail on its own.

Less obviously, both teacher and student must stand back from the school, the other students, and the art itself. Something new has been created here: Where will it fit into the ongoing process of the martial arts? A skill has been acquired and a period of apprenticeship has been finished. What now? What will the new teacher do? What will her former teacher be to her?

Often black belt students continue training and teaching in the same school. Just as often, they leave to become beginners again in another school and another art. Sometimes they start their own schools, establishing themselves immediately as head instructors.

What does the teacher do? Perhaps it is easier for her to refocus on the other students who wish to achieve advanced rank or mastery. It is also possible to quit teaching and become a beginner/non-teacher in another art. But it is also worthwhile to examine the expanded leadership possible with students-turned-teachers. Partnership in authority can be challenging, and there aren't many success stories in the history of martial arts for us to follow. Expanded leadership must include a renegotiation of what the old teacher and the new want from one another and a re-analysis of what both want from their own practice of the art. Whose students are whose? Who will pass rank? How will new ideas about the practice of the style be incorporated into the school? Can the new teacher release her old teacher from a position of authority and allow her to become a student to new ideas?

I firmly believe that many of our women's schools are very new to this last stage of the creative process. We need more dialogue and more patience with both our students coming up to join us and our older teachers seeking to redefine the art. Our new levels of mastery must be acknowledged and embraced because we are truly changing the course of martial arts training and history.

I hope this examination of teaching models can incite further dialogue and inspire awareness and insight into ourselves and our schools, so that we may continue with conscious understanding, training, teaching, and transforming ourselves: "Women training women for a better world."

AIKIDO
AND ILLUSION

Susan Perry

If you have a friend who is an Aikido student, you have probably heard some fantastic things about how Aikido has helped solve problems, problems that seemingly have nothing to do with self-defense. People find that Aikido helps them deal with harassment at the office, with a depressed daughter, with being stuck in traffic, with their colleagues, even with their ability to open a pickle jar!

The aspect of Aikido I will discuss here is what accounts for this wide range of problem solving: Cutting through illusion. I will talk about how this happens in Aikido class and why it is of particular interest to women.

Aikido differs from most other martial arts in a significant way: It offers no competition. There are no tournaments, no trophies, no ribbons or medals. Competitive activities may have their place in life, but, even in advanced Aikido practice, partners work without the ideas of winning or losing. This approach affects the feeling of practice. For example, because there is no fear of losing or desire to win, students tend knowingly and willingly to help one another improve.

Aikido does not depend on brute force but requires movement to originate from the hips. This has two wonderful consequences: Men and women can practice together, and women have a natural propensity to do Aikido well. Muscular men who have been taught to use their arm strength must constantly be reminded to relax their arms in order to practice Aikido while those women who have been discouraged from muscle building may already move naturally from their hips or center. Monthly menstrual pain and the nine-month process of childbirth alert a woman to her center. Once a woman realizes the importance of her center she begins to unleash the tremendous natural power of her body.

On the mats of an introductory Aikido class, old stereotypes abound. Some of these stereotypes clearly limit a woman in learning any self-defense. Many of us would rather be someone else. Being unhappy with who we are is a difficult issue to face. Some women don't face it, instead they pretend to be someone or something else. For example, Lucy may stride into the Aikido school sporting bold, flashy pants. To the observer, Lucy is every bit the confident extrovert she appears to be. However, just moments after entering the school, this "confident extrovert" is found shrinking back when a friendly, but large, man becomes her partner. Something is wrong here. Who Lucy wants to be is nothing like who she is. Her self-image is not accurate. Although there is no reason she can't become the confident extrovert she wishes to be, she must start at the beginning. She must clearly face who she is if she is to begin any change. Lucy needs to get herself out of the clouds and begin to work with reality.

Many women behave like Lucy. They come to Aikido class with no history of male abuse, but the moment a large man approaches as a practice partner, they suddenly feel fear and anxiety. They do not believe they are being physically intimidated, and they are surprised by their reaction. This seemingly inexplicable fear is an important issue for them because it causes them to lose control: Their relaxed and centered bodies become stiff as their focus moves up into their shoulders and neck. They develop tunnel vision and cannot move well. This fear and immobility is an issue that calls for immediate attention; moving well is critical for learning self-defense.

To add fuel to the fire, Lucy in her rigid and fearful body may be injuring her partner as she overcompensates in her move-

ments. Large men complain all the time about how small women injure them in class. Lucy may not mean anyone harm, and she may find it difficult to believe that she is hurting others, especially larger men. When Lucy is approached about the situation, she is full of denial. She cannot believe that she could hurt anyone! (Typically women believe that they do not want to hurt anyone, but often they believe they can't, that it's a physical impossibility.) Lucy's injured partners may have tried unsuccessfully to indicate to her that she is too rough. If she doesn't listen, the men in class will begin to complain about her and avoid working out with her.

The real explanation of Lucy's fear and abuse of men in class doesn't have so much to so with her male partners as they do with Lucy herself. Somewhere Lucy has fallen prey to vicious stereotypes that transform her into a monster on the Aikido mats: that a woman cannot protect herself, that a woman is not as smart as a man, that a woman is no match for someone larger than her, that a lady never gets angry or forceful, that an assertive woman will make a man angrier and thus incur greater harm, that a woman cannot injure a man, or that men do not feel pain. Lucy's partners have provided her the opportunity to recognize that something is wrong: Her assumptions, expectations, and self-image do not match what is actually happening. Although this experience is very frustrating and painful for Lucy, it can be an important and exciting time for her. Let's consider her three most likely responses.

First, if she's curious, continues to come to Aikido class, thinks about these experiences, and asks question, she begins to cut through those clouds of illusion. She will learn something about herself, and as she begins to understand the cause of her reaction, she will begin her transformation. By ridding herself of false beliefs, Lucy will begin to reclaim the tremendous power of self-esteem. On this path, Lucy becomes the confident extrovert she once pretended to be. She realizes that the movements natural to a small woman, quick turns and spins, are great self-defense tactics. This response is the hoped-for one; however, there are other, perhaps more probable, responses.

Second, Lucy may continue to attend Aikido class but refuse to admit to herself that there is any problem. She will be no fun to work with, and her partners will feel her six-foot walls of protection. Instead of working out with a nice soft body, she moves and feels like she is in a full suit of armor. If you offer a helpful criticism, her overprotective and paranoid mind will construe your attempt to help as an invasion, and you will probably get a lashing. Unfortunately, these walls that protect Lucy's self-image don't protect Lucy herself. Although Lucy remains trapped and frustrated by her illusions of how things should happen, her own prison walls prevent her from talking about it and setting things straight. It will be difficult for anyone to get through to this person; she is not dealing with reality.

Third, Lucy, when confronted with the initial fearful experience, may just pack it up and vow never to step on an Aikido mat again. This response is a real loss of opportunity for her, for there are few places where this kind of work on oneself is possible. Many distractions at home or at work interfere with the process of self-examination. On the Aikido mat, however, self-examination is hard to escape.

The process of cutting through illusion is a heady experience. In the first response, Lucy sees through her false beliefs, and by doing so she actually empowers herself. She will see that standing up for herself comes naturally and that she is her best self-protection. She will quickly find out that she needs to be careful with her Aikido partners so that she doesn't injure them.

We all live in clouds of illusion, some of us more than others. Some of us are working hard to break through these clouds, but few of us break through them all. The kinds of illusions I'm talking about have many names: stereotypes, gross generalizations, false expectations. Even one's ego or self-image is a kind of illusion. Our illusions can be about many sorts of things: the structure of the universe, the nature of human life, happiness, morality, or beauty. How often we get caught up in silly assumptions: that a physically beautiful person is also smart, that a track star must be flexible, that ethics professors are moral, or that doctors have our best interests in mind! Illusions are extremely difficult to detect. Given as gifts by our friends and family years ago, our illusions have been housed and fed for many years. They are as hard to see as an old, worn slipper under the bed.

When I was a young, idealistic graduate student on my first job, I innocently but steadfastly believed many things that seem silly to me now. I believed that ethics professors were somehow ethical (or at least tried to be) and that philosophy professors were eminently reasonable people. This cloud of illusion parted quickly when one of my academic colleagues (who was also my office mate) was accused of murder, let out of prison, and immediately asked to teach the Philosophy Department's Ethics course! Although it was an ugly reality at the time, I now thank both my murdering colleague and those other colleagues who supported his teaching for that opportunity to see my own illusions. That painful breakthrough has benefited me in many ways since.

On a more mundane level, it was in Aikido class that I learned something about the body's strength: Learning how to hold a staff taught me how to open a pickle jar. By wrapping my little finger around the jar instead of grabbing it solidly with my entire hand, I opened the jar easily. Even this is an instance of cutting through illusion: My belief about the weakness of little fingers was shown to be completely false.

Because of the cooperative nature of Aikido, I believe a woman can't progress without noticing some of her illusions, especially those common to women. When Lucy experiences her fear at the perception of a large man approaching, she is stuck with that reality. Because the practice involves no competition and no threat, Lucy must wonder why she is experiencing fear. She can claim her partner has bad intentions, that he is being competitive, that he is threatening her. But this approach does not get her far and will not work with the more senior members whom the teacher knows well. In the end Lucy has to do some digging to progress.

Illusions are particularly deep-seated things; they affect us more than we suppose. Lucy may not think she has any problems at work or at home, but do her male co-workers' and family members' perceptions of her match her own self-image? The workplace and home are not environments in which to see things clearly. There's so much going on, so much complication. But the Aikido mats help to cut through all the confusion. There is little thinking and talking, so one is discouraged from calculating and deliberating about what reaction is appropriate. However difficult this process is, it is a tremendous aid to getting a clearer view of our own reactions. If Lucy works to make her beliefs about strength and men more realistic, her Aikido will progress. Basic changes in Lucy's perceptual abilities will also go off the mat with her to the workplace and home. And things in complicated and confusing circumstances will be a little clearer as she slowly cuts her way through the clouds of illusion to reality.

WHAT IS A BLACK BELT?

Debra L. Pettis

It's a piece of material designed to go around your waist, right? Anyone can buy one, make one, or even wear one. Wrong. Anyone *can* wear one but are you characterally ready or morally ready for one? Most people feel they are physically ready no matter what shape they are in (excluding true martial artists who know differently already, regardless of rank).

Black belt is not a status once achieved that makes you invincible. It doesn't make you Superman or woman; that's comic book stuff. It doesn't make you less "afraid" in a fearful situation (granted everyone's fear level is different). It can make you able to handle that fear and use it in a constructive way.

It doesn't make you hate going to the dentist any less. Your training should help you handle the anxiety, though.

It doesn't make you any less a victim if you are, say, walking in a dark alley after dark by yourself. It doesn't mean a mugger will not attack you, hit you, or whatever. Your training should have you avoiding dark alleys after dark by yourself.

Having a black belt doesn't mean you can't bleed, can't feel pain, can't die. Don't flaunt it. Don't ask for trouble.

But at the same time don't be ashamed of all the hard work required to obtain it. Of all the mental discipline it took during your journey. Of all your sweat and yes . . . tears, I'm sure.

Frustration, pain, and happiness.

I wish I had a nickel for every time I heard, "But you're a black belt." Just because I am a black belt doesn't mean I am any less anxious when my husband gets an emergency call during the night. Again, it's how I handle it.

Black belts can break blocks and boards, and necks too, if the situation needed it. But they also should be able to comfort a child, handle grief through tears, and laugh at themselves and with others. In other words, a black belt should be a well-rounded, caring, capable human being: One who will not misuse Tae Kwon Do (or other martial arts) and who will treat her training with the responsibility and reverence, to herself and society, it deserves.

Isn't that another reason your black belt lengths are equal on each side when you tie your belt? The physical is equal to the mental.

My belt is important to me. Very. I sweated a lot for that thing. I probably would feel naked without it. But I don't feel it is as important to me as a yellow one is to a beginner. Remember when just holding your new belt was the greatest thing? Don't get me wrong on this, but at this stage of my training the physical and mental are the most important. I can see beyond the cloth (remember, anyone can buy one).

I would hope that if I never wore a belt to class that a stranger could walk in and see by my attitude and how I acted that I was indeed a true black belt.

FA JIN: TRADITIONAL CHINESE MARTIAL ARTS AND WOMEN'S SEARCH FOR EMPOWERMENT

Laurie Cahn

The study of a martial art is usually taken up for one of several reasons. The reasons may be for health or to learn to defend oneself. Martial arts practice can also be a form of artistic expression or a form of spiritual quest or inner journey. Women study the martial arts for all of these reasons, and yet for women, the underlying motivation may be the feeling of power that practice of the martial arts gives to it's most ardent devotees.

When women engage in martial arts training for health—whether it is to get some exercise, to improve flexibility and endurance, or to enhance leg or upper body strength—any improvement in these areas is apt to engender a feeling of well being and some small measure of mastery. These feelings may be unavailable or in short supply in other aspects of life, so knowing there is a place where they can be made to appear each day, however briefly, can be a source of real pride and achievement. The woman who enters a karate class never having thrown a punch and leaves an hour later having split the air with her strikes and a blood curdling *kiai* has experienced something she may have been unaware was in the realm of her physical or emotional makeup. Whether she was good at the technique, or could break a board, or repel an attacker is beside the point at this initial stage. What is important is that she experienced herself in a new way,

a way in which she could sense her potential power. The woman who wants to learn to defend herself and takes a self-defense class, learns a simple wrist lock in a Judo class, or finds out that she can fall and not get hurt in her first Aikido class has experienced some small victories that may let her walk down the street with her head up, because she no longer feels so much the victim.

Practicing a solo form in a class or alone in a park lets a woman feel expressive and competent in a field where her only opponent is herself or whomever she chooses to envision. She can feel beautiful, strong, and flexible and can create her own arena for whatever expression she selects. Martial art is an accurate term not just for those masters whose ability has transcended the mundane and reached a higher plane, but also for anyone who is striving for beauty and self-expression in their chosen form.

In the West particularly, some may seek out the martial arts as a path to self-realization or discovery. Some may be looking for a mother or father figure, which the teacher supplies (willingly or not). Others may use their training as a path to self-enlightenment. In Japanese arts the word *do*, which follows certain styles, means "the way." Likewise in Chinese arts the word *quan* can denote not only the word fist, but also an entire school or mode of thought. Some Chinese styles such as *Taiji Quan* and *Bagua Zhang* even carry in their names philosophical concepts that resonate with deep meaning for those familiar with classical Chinese philosophy and world view. But for all the reasons we have examined that women choose to study martial arts, what special relevance do these reasons have to traditional Chinese martial arts, and what do these arts have to offer women in particular?

I have often noticed that many more women study Japanese and Korean arts than study traditional Chinese arts, and I'd like to examine this phenomenon. In the Bay Area, which is home to a flourishing women's martial arts community, there are women's schools of Aikido, Kajukenbo, Kenpo, Judo, Jujitsu, and Naginata. Not one exclusively women's school teaches traditional Chinese martial arts. In fact in my travels around the country, I have yet to see an all women's Chinese martial art school. There are some extraordinary women teachers, Professor Wang Jurong in Houston comes immediately to mind, but these women are likely to have as many, or more, male than female students.

Why do Chinese martial arts seem less attractive to women? Part of the reason may be found in the term that is synonymous with Chinese martial arts in the west: *kung fu*. In China there are many different terms for martial arts, but the most common is *wushu*, which literally translated means war arts or techniques. The term kung fu is used, particularly in the Southern parts of China, to refer to martial arts, but kung fu actually applies to any art of skill that is acquired after a great investment of time and energy. Kung fu means that you have gone beyond the surface of your chosen art or craft and reached a deeper level or understanding and ability. This concept is at odds with the typical American mind that values speed and efficiency above all else.

In most Japanese or Korean empty-hand martial art classes, a beginning student learns the rudiments of punching or kicking soon after signing up. Punching and kicking with power is emphasized right away, and students are encouraged to punch "harder" and to kick powerfully and quickly. This method of training can build strength and power quickly, and for women, it can satisfy an immediate need to feel powerful and strong. This feeling can be instrumental in helping a woman change her self-image and begin to feel her potential power in both the physical and metaphysical arenas.

A traditional Chinese martial arts class does not usually offer such immediate gratification. When students learn to punch they are not urged to punch with power, they are encouraged to relax, to forget power, to try to feel their whole body, not just their arms. Much emphasis may also be placed on stances. While her karate counterpart is punching harder and kicking more powerfully, the kung fu beginner is told to sit down lower, relax, and forget about issuing power. To a beginner, this is often confusing and sometimes disheartening. She may feel envious, she may even quit.

What is behind this peculiarly Chinese method of training? My first class as a "new beginner" with my teacher might shed some light on this contradictory aspect of traditional Chinese methods of training. When I decided to change schools and styles ten years ago, I had already been training in a Chinese martial art for ten years. I had been the chief instructor of a branch of my former teacher's school, I'd done lots of sparring and kick boxing and was thought to be proficient. I had also felt that my practice had begun to stagnate, I knew I needed a new teacher who could take me to a different level. When I arrived at class that first night, I was aware that the senior students, all men, regarded me as an unwelcome interloper into their previously all-male domain. I was determined to show them, and my new teacher, that I could do it. I wanted to show how tough and strong I was. I was instructed to follow one of the senior students, who was, of course, the most arrogant and annoying one, across the backyard doing a simple punching technique. I put as much power as I could into each punch, straining with effort, trying to match, and even best, my partner's movement. When we finished, my teacher beckoned to me and dismissed the other student. I waited to hear the verdict.

"Well," he said, "you're pretty strong." (Inside I was beaming!) "But," (uh oh, I sensed this 'but' could be leading to trouble ...) "what you do, you could do sitting in a chair." (Say what? Now, I was totally and completely confused.) "If you want to leave here right now," he went on, "with your kind of body movement, you could learn karate much more easily than kung fu. You can be really good at karate right now, if you like. But if you want to do kung fu, you have to wash away all your old movements. You have to become like a baby." He paused, "Well?"

I assured him that I didn't want to do karate, that it was kung fu that I wanted, and that I was completely willing to wash, boil, or disinfect all my old habits if that was what it would take. He said, "Good," and that was the beginning of a journey that continues to this day.

I didn't understand at first what my teacher meant by "becoming like a baby." To a feminist, acting like a baby seems the opposite of everything that the women's movement had tried to achieve. Yet, as time went on I began to understand.

When my teacher said that what I was doing, I could do in a chair, he meant that Chinese kung fu requires you to use your entire body when executing a technique, even a simple punch. In fact, the Chinese often say, "The whole body is a fist." Some kung fu styles put it differently saying they have seven "fists." (These include the head, shoulder, elbow, hand, hip, knee, and foot.) I had been using only my arms, with some occasional help from my waist.

I began to see that where the ideal Western body type could be said to be shaped like an inverted (▼) triangle with broad shoulders atop a small, tapered waist that fed into long slim legs; the typical Chinese body type turned the triangle upside down (▲). The upper body was often small and flat, with long ropey muscles, not the Ramboesque bulk that so many Westerners aspire to. Most important was the legs, which were short and powerful. Now, as most women know, the only American woman who is built like the inverted triangle is Barbie; the rest of us are probably closer to the Chinese triangle model. For many of us our bodies are almost ideally suited for Chinese martial arts! As someone who has a long body and short legs, I began to feel for the first time, that I was doing something where my body was an asset!

So, what about the baby? When you are used to doing something one way, and you have some success with that method, you continue, following the old American adage, "If it ain't broke, don't fix it." I'd used my upper body, and it worked for me, but now my teacher wanted me to give that up and do it his way. 'His way' meant that I was required to relax, that I had to learn to use my legs, hips, and waist to drive my arms. This meant instead of feeling strong and competent, I was reduced to feeling weak and inept. I hated it! And yet I knew that it was the only way to change. The more I relaxed, the weaker I felt, but the more my teacher seemed to feel that I was improving. Bizarre.... And yet as time passed, I felt myself grow stronger than I'd been, both in my body and my mind.

I began to feel that I could *fa jin:* issue power.

Fa jin is a term worth examining. Several terms in Chinese refer to power, but here *jin* is the important concept. *Jin* is not just power, but a special energy or force, one that is lively and spirited and contains all your essential elements. When you *fa jin*, you use everything at your disposal, you don't hold back. Everything that is inside, comes out, meaning you maximize all your potential for power. This metaphor is perfect for what women ultimately want from martial arts practice: to be able to reach and use all the possible power that resides in their bodies, minds, and spirits.

And that is the real lesson.

Becoming a baby turns out to be a great thing because ultimately babies are fearless, open, unafraid, and pure. A baby doesn't worry about what other people think (Do I look weak? Am I strong?). A baby uses its entire body in a completely relaxed manner to achieve it's goals. Of course, a baby doesn't have the coordination or strength of an adult, but then neither does a baby have the inhibitions or tensions that hamper our bodies and minds as adults.

Traditional training in a Chinese martial art has lessons that can be especially valuable to women. Yet, so often women dismiss the traditional methods of practice out of frustration or misunderstanding.

Any martial art can benefit a dedicated practitioner—the great thing about training is that you get out of it exactly what you put in. I urge women not to dismiss the Chinese martial arts as too soft, too fancy, or with too much emphasis on form. Because, after all, aren't these the very same arguments that have been used to dismiss women for years?

CLEARING THE WAY
FOR FREEDOM

Janet E. Aalfs

I. A Life Worth Living

I am a black belt woman, student of a black belt woman, with black belt women students of my own who now have their own students. Four generations of women teaching women. A legacy of victories and disappointments. I am all that has come before me, all that follows—strands of energy spiralling together symbolized by the belt I wear that frays with time, exposing the self I learn to cherish and protect.

I see before me the struggles of my teacher, the effects of training in a male-dominated setting, the triumphs of her journey, and the damage caused by abuse and isolation. I see after me the struggles of my students, their successes and difficulties in expressing the pain and joy of their deepest selves. I have learned to trust in my relationships with my teachers, peers, and students that I am acting out of love when I refuse to accept abusive behavior or any rationalization for it.

I want to believe that studying martial arts is, in and of itself, transformative. That the energy of a form is automatically healing. That women training in martial arts will, by the very miracle of our presence, reinvent the world. All this is true and not true. Martial arts can be practiced with integrity or can be misused, like anything. My sense of responsibility—the ability to respond —to myself, the arts, and all forms of life increases as I become more aware of positive ways to use the power inside and around me. I feel compelled to remind:

- It is not o.k. to hurt ourselves or each other, physically, emotionally, or spiritually, in the name of "getting tough."
- It is not o.k. to play favorites with some and scapegoat others, pitting one against the other in the name of "achievement."
- It is not o.k. to punish students in the name of "developing discipline."
- It is not o.k. to be silent or ignorant about the racism, ableism, ageism, classism, etc. that is present within our schools and training environments in the name of "we're all sisters here."

Abuse is not o.k. Period.

We, as women martial artists, have made incredible progress in being honest with ourselves and each other. We have scheduled workshops and workouts to address issues of oppression. We have expanded our visions of excellence to include women with disabilities. We have increased our awareness of the achievements of old women. We have broken down barriers between styles and types of martial arts and dared to be the best we can be. Still, we have a long way to go in examining our own self-abusive patterns and ways of taking out our anger and frustrations on each other. I am constantly challenged to return to myself: What part do I play in this process?

The koan given to me by my teacher, "A life unexamined is not worth living," now goes, "A life well-examined is worth living." This example, though seemingly small, symbolizes for me an important gift that is enhanced through training in the martial arts: an improved ability to redirect energy and to see the positive side of what appears in a negative form.

I began in martial arts afraid that I had no public voice, that I was doomed, as was true in my biological family, to stand by and silently witness people I cared about ripping each other apart. If I were spared, it was only for the moment and due to pure luck. I feared that if I spoke out, I would either be ignored or sucked

into the bottomless pit of pain. I asked my teacher in the early stages of my training why she yelled at most of the other students but not at me. She said she didn't have to yell at me, that I didn't do anything to make her yell. My next question was why she had to yell at anyone, like she had no choice.

I forgive my teacher. I forgive myself for the mistakes I have made and the times I have lacked the courage of my convictions. I have compassion for the risks my students take to communicate with me and forgive them when they cannot. Forgiveness is a state of grace. I thank whatever gives me the strength to let go of what is no longer useful to me, and I am grateful for all the ways that people I care about hang in there when the road is rough. My life is worth living because the love I feel grows the more I express it. I challenge myself and others, with love, to dare to question even the smallest occurrences of abusive behavior and to congratulate ourselves for acting responsibly—to make ourselves better.

II. The Ways of Pine Trees and Rattan

The pine tree, which "bends but does not break," symbolizes Shuri-ryu karate, a style spread throughout the U.S. by the late Grandmaster Robert A. Trias, teacher of my teacher. Modern Arnis, developed by Grandmaster Remy Presas who came from the Philippines to share this art, uses rattan canes that are highly flexible and durable. The interweaving of these two martial arts inspires spontaneity and openmindedness. In my practice, I am challenged to expand my understanding of both arts to experience more fully their similarities and differences. In combining these two arts, the whole equals more than the sum of the parts.

Both Shuri and Arnis have long and complicated histories. There are more than 7,000 styles of Filipino stickfighting. The word "arnis" is said to have come from *arnes*, Spanish for harness, part of a costume used in Filipino religious plays known as *moro-moro*, where stickfighting was kept alive when outlawed by conquerors.[1] Shuri-ryu, meaning "beautiful and graceful," developed in Okinawa with influences from other countries (including India, China, and Japan). Weapons were outlawed at various times in Okinawa's history, which led the people to defend themselves against oppressive regimes with their hands, feet, and farm implements. Okinawa was the home of *Noros*, shamanic women who created and practiced the rituals and techniques handed down to us through an often denied and erased martial arts herstory.

One of the "23 Ways to Recognize the Shuri-ryu System" is its 90% circular movement.[2] Forearm rotation gives strength to every strike. The spiralling of the spine, beginning in the hips, connects the upper to lower body and infuses every movement with momentum and power. The basis for movement in Arnis is the figure-8, the symbol of infinity. *Sinawalis* are striking and blocking exercises done with the cane or empty hands. The name for these weaving patterns comes from the woven bamboo matting used as walls in the Philippines. This constant spiralling develops FLOW and RELAXATION, which are essential elements of FLEXIBILITY. The foundation for all of this is BREATH.

In teaching a combination of Shuri and Arnis, I have felt my flow develop and grow. It is helpful to be able to learn about one system from the perspective of another. Grandmaster Presas teaches Arnis as "the art within your art." He encourages his students to use the concepts of Arnis in understanding other martial arts and vice versa, and in understanding life in general. His

---

[1] Presas, Remy, *Modern Arnis.*
[2] Trias, Robert A., *The Pinnacle of Karate.*

background includes the study of Judo, Jiu-jitsu, and karate. Grandmaster Trias practiced a variety of forms over time and brought together people of many karate styles through the United States Karate Association, an organization he founded. Another organization, the National Women's Martial Arts Federation, now almost twenty years old, encourages women to share our arts with each other for the benefit of all. In their differences, certain concepts are basic to any of the arts.

Flexibility on all levels—physical, mental, and spiritual—is one of the basic elements that any martial artist must learn and practice to progress in her training. Each woman has her unique situation and style and each learns in her own special way. The word flexibility means capable of being flexed (moved, bent), yielding to influence, capable of responding or conforming to changing or new situations.[3] To some, this may seem like being pushed around or succumbing to another's whim. My idea of flexibility is one where I am able to respond in a positive and creative way (or choose not to respond), regardless of the circumstances. I may not have a choice about what happens to and around me, but I do have a choice about what actions I take in any given situation. Knowing that I can create options for myself and others helps give me a sense of power in my life.

To develop flexibility of body—practice. To develop flexibility of mind—practice. To develop flexibility of spirit—practice. Make this practice a beautiful *sinawali*, each strand adding to the strength of the whole.

III. *Shu*—To Learn from Tradition, *Ri*—To Go Beyond, Excel

I have been thinking and feeling a lot over time about the concept of multiplicity, that is, many realities existing in the same moment. Because each of us comes from different circumstances and has specific and unique needs, no single program could possibly encompass all of us. However, we all have certain things in common—we are human beings, we are women and children,

---

[3]Webster's New Collegiate Dictionary.

we have all experienced some level of abuse/violence in our lives that takes particular forms depending on who we are, we are at Valley Women's Martial Arts (or wherever) to face that violence and turn our fear and anger into energy that we can use in healthy ways. I operate on the assumption that what we each gain individually benefits all of us and in turn affects the rest of the world—the women, men, and children with whom we come in contact. Each of us is responsible for how she uses any skill she acquires. "Karate is my secret. I bear no weapons. I accept responsibility for my actions and ask for forgiveness." These are hidden spiritual meanings of the opening and closing moves of every *kata* we perform.

As a teacher, I share my knowledge with those who ask for it and are willing to engage in an honest and compassionate relationship with themselves and me. When people misuse this process or are not ready for the commitment for whatever reason, they usually don't get very far. My concept of the teacher/student relationship is that it is basically about increasing communication skills on physical/mental/spiritual planes to facilitate the process of sharing and letting go. Loving myself, other people, and the practice of the martial arts requires the ability to share in non-judgemental, unconditional ways and to accept where I have influence and where I do not.

For me, part of having opinions and beliefs is recognizing that others also have their own and that this will, at times, lead to disagreement. Discord does not have to be negative, but we have been taught to be afraid of it and have not been certain that our strong opinions and beliefs are as valid as the next person's. As a leader, I am constantly weighing what I see as the good of the whole against my personal needs/desires/commitments. As a follower, I seek out those whose teachings and leadership I trust in order to learn from them.

What we see happening in front of our eyes has roots in the past and results in the future. Nothing is new under the sun. However, transformation does happen. One thing becomes another. Similar issues arise time and again and we keep finding new strengths and attitudes to deal more healthily with what passes our way. I have seen these transformations occur over the years, and I experience the source of them as love—for and from myself, others, the arts, the world. This is what gives me hope.

I consider it my responsibility to respond to the question "How do I use what I learn in martial arts both inside and outside the *dojo?*" My responses are shaped by various factors, including my race, age, gender, physical ability, sexual preference, class, religion, size, mental ability, which all affect how oppressed or oppressive I am. I don't expect my choices of how to deal with these struggles to be the same as someone else's and I don't appreciate it when someone else tries to force his or her choices on me. One way I use what I learn is to constantly challenge any dogma I encounter. Dogma exists in every realm—neither martial artists nor feminists are immune to proselytizing. By dogma I mean any beliefs that are put forth as "the answers" or "the right way" or "politically correct." The strength of Valley Women's Martial Arts lies in the diversity of its members, the abilities of each of us to make her voice heard, and the fact that we are women and children together reclaiming our power. The challenge is to take advantage of the available opportunities to clear the way for freedom for every form of life on earth.

The Way of the Crane[4]

Crane dances
because she loves to

not to attract
a mate

or scare
a foe

not for anyone else
though when she wants

she suspends herself
in the raven-blue sky

wings shining light
as a prayer

looms over my head
eclipsing the moon

elusive as wind
she waits for me

I hear her
high-pitched song

shiver through bone
and spread my arms

palms open to night
lifting

---

[4]The crane is one of the five animals of Shuri-ryu. The other four are tiger, leopard, dragon and snake.

WOMEN, POWER, AND EMPOWERMENT

Elizabeth Hendricks

Power is a provocative word. It conjures up images of authority, of dominance, and of forcefulness. The dictionary describes power as the ability to "do something" or to "do anything." To have power is to act upon something or someone strongly. Many women today seem to have a certain amount of confusion over this concept of power. For some women, power has a secondary, more subtle meaning: It translates as "something that I am not allowed to have." Women frequently perceive power as belonging in the exclusive domain of men and see power as a foreign entity that has a "No Women Allowed" sign posted on it. These women misidentify power as an essentially masculine reality and may come to believe they must be powerful in the same way that men are powerful.

Most martial arts are still dominated by men. In most Aikido *dojos* one still finds more men than women training. The unfortunate reality is that there are relatively few women of high rank. Even when one allows for the larger number of men than women who train, a significant disparity still exists between the number of high ranking men and women. It is easy to come up with the names of men who have attained the rank of Godan (fifth degree black belt) or above. By contrast, very few women have been awarded these ranks. As a result, most role models at the highest

134

ranks are men. It is from role models that a student learns "what is the correct way to BE a good Aikidoist." All students take cues from their instructors in learning how to perform their Aikido and attempt to execute their Aikido just as their instructors do. In terms of technique, imitating the teacher is a valid way to learn and practice. But what happens when the teacher is a man and the student is a woman?

The woman may identify with her male teacher (understandable in any student) and try in all ways to imitate him. This imitation may include not only imitating the teacher's technique but also may extend to blind imitation of the teacher's personal style. The obvious hazard for the woman student is that she may attempt to do her Aikido like a man. She may not even consider the possibility that strong Aikido done by a woman might be somewhat different than strong Aikido done by a man. Thus the adaptation of trying to perform or relate to Aikido in a masculine way is not a conscious decision. Often the woman is just doing her best to copy her teacher and to be a good and sincere student. To imitate the teacher is a legitimate way to learn and perform Aikido; however, when a woman adopts a masculine way of being on the mat rather than her own natural (female) way of being an Aikidoist, she loses something very valuable. She loses authenticity in how she handles herself in terms of personal power.

It is understandable that women might perceive power as having a masculine flavor. Many world cultures are structured in a way that men are the ones who have access to powerful positions in government, in industry, and so on. In our society, women are still frequently relegated to the back seat in organizations, with less voice in the determination of the really important decisions. Women are still underrepresented in management positions in business and have a much harder time finding mentors to help them advance their careers.

Of course, the Women's Movement helped expand the roles women could take. In the 60's, women began to learn it was possible for them to enter areas that were previously considered "off limits" and compete with men. But often women were taught

that the way to succeed in these fields was by aping men. Women were advised that dressing for success meant wearing a suit (remember pant-suits in the 60's?) in order to resemble a man. Presumably this meant that those in authority (men) might take the woman more seriously if she looked just like them. Women were trained that to get to the top meant they had to suppress their feminine side and cultivate their masculine skills. This training was a great disservice to women, because the feminine way of processing information and dealing with choices and decisions is just as valid as the masculine way. It is different, that's all!

We have come a long way since then. Women are out in the world in many different occupations and are having great success at these jobs. More and more one can see successful women who are not intimidated into copying men. These women are able to be female at the same time they are engaging in all kinds of jobs. However, I see remnants of the idea "power equals male" in many women Aikidoists I have met and trained with.

This idea can lead a woman to make a certain kind of psychological adaptation: She comes to believe she can only be powerful when she operates in a male or macho way, which can lead her to the conclusion: "It is not possible to be feminine and to be powerful." Softness may be equated with vulnerability while receptivity may feel like laying herself open to being victimized.

A woman operating with this concept may attempt to execute her Aikido like a man in the sincere belief that this is the only way in which she can be strong. She also may discover that this is the only way she will be taken as a serious student in her *dojo.*

Once a woman has concluded that male equals power and female implies lack of power, she may also come to believe that she is weak; just as women were known as "the weaker sex" for many years. This belief that "I'm a woman, and therefore I am weak" may be experienced as a belief that one is weak physically, a belief that one is weak psychologically, or both. A woman who holds such a world view is sometimes tentative about getting on the mat and may be anxious about getting hurt during practice. Such a woman may not think she can handle an arduous practice. Indeed, women with this cognitive structure often radically underestimate their capabilities in the *dojo.* One of our students once said to me (in response to my request that she execute her throws with more assurance and authority), "I can't throw Kevin hard, after all, I'm just a woman."

This belief that to be powerful one must operate in a masculine mode separates the woman from her source of grounding and empowerment. For example, intuition is considered to be a "right brain" (feminine) characteristic. Intuition is invaluable in the martial arts, for intuition tells us that our partner is going to attack before he or she moves. If we know intuitively where an opponent is likely to move, we can then direct his or her energy and neutralize the attack. In Aikido it is important to be able to feel our opponent's *ki* movement . . . and feeling is the domain of the feminine. A woman who believes she must suppress her feminine side in how she does her martial arts has sacrificed contact with a wealth of important and useful information. This does not mean that the woman should abandon her connection with traits that have been associated with the masculine. To be well rounded as an Aikidoist, one would ideally have a good connection with the qualities associated with the feminine and also with the logical, linear side associated with the masculine.

What might be helpful in freeing women from a belief system that constricts their self-concept as potent, empowered individuals in their own right? Women could be exposed to new information that would call into question their old beliefs that they cannot be empowered as women and as Aikidoists. They need to see, over and over, that it is possible for a woman to function in the feminine mode at the same time she is functioning well as a martial artist. Some women are amazed to see senior women who do have a sense of authority as women in their Aikido. You can almost see wheels racing around inside their heads as they ingest the idea that Power can also equal Female! Once their perception has made this quantum shift, it is a delight to witness a real transformation in these women. Sometimes they will laugh with both pleasure and amazement as they dispatch their partners to the floor. One of our students wound up jumping up and down with excitement, proclaiming "WOW! I'M POWERFUL!" as she went down a Randori line flinging people left and right. She was throwing strongly but with rhythm and sensitivity at the same time.

Aikido is wonderfully empowering for women, for it teaches us how to be grounded in our own being while executing physical movements. Aikido is based on circles and spirals and demonstrates beautifully that Yin energy is potent. Yin, the dark feminine, accepts; it is receptive without being "wimpy"; it contains great energy. Yang, the masculine, is associated with logic and with "doing." Both are necessary for balance. In Aikido women can see the power of the Yin/Yang dance, and they learn they can ground themselves and dance in that arena. Women should not have to imitate men nor should they have to act macho to be taken seriously (or to take themselves seriously). To dance on that border between the two opposites and to accept both sides as valid is to accept ourselves for what we really are . . . empowered.

ABOUT THE CONTRIBUTORS

Janet Aalfs holds a third degree black belt in Shuri-ryu (Okinawan Karate) and a third degree black belt in Arnis (Filipino Stick-fighting). Since 1982 she has been a head instructor of Valley Women's Martial Arts, Inc. in western Massachusetts. She is also a poet and fiction writer whose work has been published in feminist and lesbian/gay journals and anthologies.

Laurie Cahn has studied the Chinese martial arts for twenty years and currently teaches in San Francisco, Ca. For the last ten years she has studied a variety of traditional northern styles and weapons with Master Adam Hsu. She is also a writer and had her own column, "The Yin Perspective," in *Black Belt Magazine.*

Jody Curley has studied T'ai Chi Ch'uan since 1982. She received her certification in 1989 from Master William C. C. Chen and currently teaches at the T'ai Chi Ch'uan Association of Indiana, Inc. She also has a master's degree in counseling psychology and creative writing and works with older adults and their families.

Ellie Doermann has studied the martial arts since 1982 and currently trains in Northern Shaolin Kung Fu. She is a physical therapist who says that she works with people who continually teach her that whatever our abilities to move and whatever our chances to survive, we will always be warriors.

Maria Doest is a fourth degree black belt in Okinawan Shorin-ryu Karate and has been teaching since 1974. She is currently Chief Instructor of KarateWomen School in Los Angeles, Ca. In 1987 Maria took the first women's fighting team to Japan where they captured the gold medal at the All-Japan Friendship Koshiki Tournament. Maria is also a stuntwoman and fight scene coordinator who enjoys using her skills in the martial arts to change the way women are depicted in film when confronting violence.

Michelle Dwyer has studied the Chinese martial arts in the San Francisco Bay Area for sixteen years and has been a teacher for nine years. She has also studied Yoga and Aikido.

Janet Gee has studied the martial arts since 1971, primarily Choy Li Fut Kung Fu and T'ai Chi Ch'uan, although she has also trained in Aikido, Tae Kwon Do, Judo, and Kempo Karate. She is the founder and director of Janet Gee's Martial Arts Training in San Francisco, Ca. and conducts workshops throughout the United States, Australia, and Europe.

Karla Grant has studied the martial arts since 1973. She holds a fifth degree black belt in Kenpo Karate and a third degree black belt in Kosho-Shorei Karate. She teaches martial arts and self-defense for the public and private sectors as a consultant/lecturer through the Shinko Learning Center in Sacramento, Ca.

Elizabeth Hendricks has pursued martial arts training for eleven years and has been training in Aikido since 1983. She currently teaches and trains in Portland, Oregon and writes a column on *dojo* conflicts for *Aikido Today Magazine*. She also holds a doctorate in psychology and is in private practice working with women survivors of abuse.

Kathy Hopwood has studied the martial arts since 1972, training in Tae Kwon Do, Shorin-ryu, Hung Gar Kung Fu, and Modern Arnis. She is the founder of Triangle Women's Martial Arts Center in Durham, N.C. and a partner in SafeSkills Associates, which offers self-defense programs to universities and businesses.

Debby Kirkman has studied the Burmese martial art of Bando since 1984 and holds a first degree black belt test. She also holds a first degree black belt in Tae Kwon Do and works as a systems engineer in the aviation industry.

Valerie Lee is an acupuncturist and a long-time student of the Chinese martial arts.

Debbie Leung has studied the martial arts since 1978 and Northern Shaolin Kung Fu since 1981. She is a self-defense instructor and co-founder of Feminists in Self-Defense Training (FIST) in Olympia Wa. She is also the author of *Self-Defense: The Womanly Art of Self-Care, Intuition, and Choice,* published by R&M Press in 1991.

Marilyn May holds a second degree black belt in Tae Kwon Do. She recently began training in Cuong Nhu, a Vietmanese eclectic martial art. She is also a therapist who works with adolescents, children, and families.

Anne Moon has studied the martial arts since 1973. She holds a second degree black belt in Kajukenbo and a first degree black belt in Modern Arnis and has also studied Pa Kua Chang and Laban Movement Analysis. She is the founder and chief instructor of Seven Star Women's Kung Fu in Seattle, Wa.

Wendy Palmer has studied Aikido for twenty years and holds a third degree black belt. She is an instructor at Tamalpais Aikido in Mill Valley, Ca.

Susan Perry has trained in Aikido for 14 years. She and her husband founded the Claremont Colleges Aikido Club and Musubi Dojo in Upland, Ca., where she currently teaches Aikido. Susan has a Ph.D. in Philosophy and is also the co-founder of Arete Press and the editor of *Aikido Today Magazine.*

Debra L. Pettis has a third degree black belt in the Chang Moo Kwan style of Tae Kwon Do. She is an instructor and the co-owner of Theodore Tae Kwon Do, Inc. in Theodore, Alabama. She is also the new owner/editor of the magazine, *Fighting Woman News.*

Deborah Wheeler studied T'ai Chi Ch'uan for four years then began training in Kung Fu San Soo, which she has studied for sixteen years and in which she holds a fifth degree black belt. Deborah is a writer who has published a number of short stories and whose first novel, *Jaydium,* will be published by DAW Books.

Wendy Whited has studied the martial arts for 18 years, beginning with Judo and including karate and Iaido. Her main art is Aikido, in which she holds a fourth degree black belt. She lived in Japan for two years and studied at Hombu Dojo, the world headquarters of Aikido.

Carol A. Wiley has trained in the martial arts since 1979. She holds a second degree black belt in Tae Kwon Do and currently trains in Aikido. Carol is also a writer and editor.

Lidia Alexandra Wolanskyj began training in Aikido with Massimo di Villadorata (Montreal Aikikai) in 1972. She founded Pacific Aikido Kensankai Association in Vancouver, British Columbia, where she taught until 1987. She has trained in Japan and Europe and across Canada and the U.S. In the fall of 1991, she was part of a teaching team in Kiev and Moscow. Lidia is also a writer and editor.

Lydia Zijdel (a paraplegic since 1982) has studied Aikido and Shuri-ryu Karate in Amsterdam, The Netherlands since 1985. She holds a first degree black belt in Shuri-ryu Karate. She is a licensed self-defense teacher and developed a Teachers Training Course for martial arts teachers who want to open their classes to people with disabilities.

FURTHER READING

Self-Defense and Rape Prevention

Bart, Pauline B. and Patricia H. O'Brien, *Stopping Rape: Successful Survival Strategies*, Pergamon Press, 1985.

Bateman, Py, *Fear into Anger*, Nelson-Hall, 1978.

— Caignon, Denise and Gail Grove, *Her Wits About Her: Self-Defense Stories by Women*, Harper and Row, 1987.

Delacoste, Frederique and Felice Newman, ed., *Fight Back! Feminist Resistance to Male Violence*, Cleis Press, 1981.

Leung, Debbie, *The Womanly Art of Self-Care, Intuition, and Choice*, R&M Press, 1991.

Monkerud, Donald and Mary Heiny, *Self-Defense for Women*, William C. Brown Publishers, 1980.

Nelson, Joan M., *Self-Defense: Steps to Success*, Leisure Press, 1991.

Sanford, Linda Tschirhart and Ann Fetter, *In Defense of Ourselves: A Rape Prevention Handbook for Women*, Doubleday and Company, 1979.

Smith, Susan E., *Fear or Freedom: A Woman's Options in Social Survival & Physical Defense*, Mother Courage Press, 1986.

The Martial Arts

Almeida, Bira, *Capoeira: A Brazilian Art Form*, North Atlantic Books, 1986.

Atkinson, Linda, *Women in the Martial Arts: A New Spirit Rising*, Dodd, Mead and Company, 1983.

Chow, David and Richard Spangler, *Kung Fu: History, Philosophy, and Technique*, Unique Publications, 1982.

Deshimaru, Taisen, *The Zen Way to the Martial Arts*, E. P. Dutton, 1982.

Draeger, Donn F. and Robert W. Smith, *Asian Fighting Arts*, Berkley Publishing Corporation, 1974.

Heckler, Richard Strozzi, ed., *Aikido and the New Warrior*, North Atlantic Books, 1985.

Inosanto, Dan, *The Filipino Martial Arts*, Know Now Publishing Company, 1980.

Kauz, Herman, *The Martial Spirit*, The Overlook Press, 1977.

Nelson, Randy, ed., *Overlook Martial Arts Reader: Classic Writings on Philosophy and Technique*, The Overlook Press, 1989.

Nelson, Randy with Katherine C. Whittaker, *The Martial Arts: An Annotated Bibliography*, The Overlook Press, 1988.

Payne, Peter, *Martial Arts: The Spiritual Dimension*, Thames and Hudson, Ltd., London, 1981.

Ratti, Oscar and Adele Westbrook, *Secrets of the Samurai: The Martial Arts of Feudal Japan*, Charles E. Tuttle Co., 1973.

Reid, Howard and Michael Croucher, *The Way of the Warrior: The Paradox of the Martial Arts*, The Overlook Press, 1991.

Ribner, Susan and Dr. Richard Chin, *The Martial Arts*, Harper and Row, 1978.

Saotome, Mitsugi, *Principles of Aikido*, Shambhala Publications, 1989.

Stevens, John, *Aikido: The Way of Harmony*, Shambhala Publications, 1984.

Ueshiba, Kisshomaru, *The Spirit of Aikido*, Kodansha International, 1984.

Ueshiba, Morihei, *Budo: Teachings of the Founder of Aikido*, Kodansha International, 1991.

Warner, Gordon and Donn F. Draeger, *Japanese Swordsmanship: Technique and Practice*, Weatherhill, 1982.

Westbrook, Adele and Oscar Ratti, *Aikido and the Dynamic Sphere*, Charles E. Tuttle Co., 1970.

White, Thomas M., *Three Golden Pearls on a String: The Esoteric Teachings of Karate-Do and the Mystical Journey of a Warrior Priest*, North Atlantic Books, 1991.

Other Books of Interest

Crum, Thomas F., *The Magic of Conflict*, Simon and Schuster, 1987.

Hoff, Benjamin, *The Tao of Pooh*, Penguin Books, 1982.

Kim, Tae Yun, *Seven Steps to Inner Power: A Martial Arts Master Reveals Her Secrets for Dynamic Living*, New World Library, 1991.

Lao-tzu, *Tao Te Ching*, various translations available.

Pater, Robert, *The Black-Belt Manager: Martial Arts Strategies for*